Egypt from Independence to Revolution, 1919-1952

CONTEMPORARY ISSUES IN THE MIDDLE EAST

SELMA BOTMAN

Egypt from Independence to Revolution, 1919-1952

SYRACUSE UNIVERSITY PRESS

First Edition
91 92 93 94 95 96 97 98 99   6 5 4 3 2 1

The paper used in this publication meets the minimum
requirements of American National Standard for Information Sciences—Permanence of Paper for Printed Library
Materials, ANSI Z39.48-1984.

Library of Congress Cataloging-in-Publication Data
Botman, Selma.
   Egypt from independence to revolution, 1919–1952 /
Selma Botman.
      p.   cm. — (Contemporary issues in the Middle East)
   Includes bibliographical references and index.
   ISBN 0-8156-2530-8 (cloth). — ISBN 0-8156-2531-6 (paper)
   1. Egypt—History—1919- I. Title. II. Series.
   DT107.B58   1991
   962.05—dc20   91-7246

Manufactured in the United States of America

A healthy nation is as unconscious of its nationality as a healthy man of his bones. But if you break a nation's nationality it will think of nothing else but getting it set again. It will listen to no reformer, to no philosopher, to no preacher, until the demand of the Nationalist is granted. It will attend to no business, however vital, except the business of unification and liberation.

GEORGE BERNARD SHAW in the "Preface for Politicians" preceding his play *John Bull's Other Island*, 1916 edition

for my mother, Gertrude Botman

Selma Botman, author of *The Rise of Egyptian Communism, 1939-1970* (Syracuse University Press), is Assistant Professor of Political Science at the College of the Holy Cross. She has been a contributor to *Studies in Comparative Communism, Middle Eastern Studies, Journal of South Asian and Middle Eastern Studies, Immigrants and Minorities,* and *Women's Studies International Forum.*

Contents

Illustrations

Tables

Maps

Acknowledgments

I would like to thank the many people who inspired and aided in the publication of this book. In particular, I extend heartfelt gratitude to Albert Hourani, John Esposito, John Voll, Peter Gran, Zachary Lockman, Lena Jayyusi, Janet Grenzke, David Schaefer, Kathleen Beaulieu, and Theodore Constan. I would also like to acknowledge the members of my family who have helped me in innumerable ways throughout the writing and researching of this book. In particular, I extend my appreciation to Nancy Birmingham, who accompanied me on a trip to Egypt during the summer of 1986 and encouraged me to look at the country in new and insightful ways. My husband, Tom Birmingham, as always has contributed his talents to this project. To my mother, Gertrude Botman, to whom this book is dedicated, I owe an enormous debt of gratitude, and I deeply appreciate her steady encouragement and her untiring assistance.

I am grateful to the National Endowment for the Humanities, the American Research Center in Egypt, and the College of the Holy Cross for making my research possible. The Center for Middle Eastern Studies at Harvard University has graciously allowed me access to the resources of the university's libraries. Mary Ellen Taylor, Photo Archivist at the Harvard Semitic Museum, kindly made me aware of a variety of photographic collections on the Middle East. Upon her suggestion, I acquired photographs from the G. Eric Matson Collection housed at the Library of Congress in Washington, D.C. I extend thanks to the Episcopal Home in Alhambra, California, for allowing me to use photos from the Matson Collection.

I am grateful to the estate of George Bernard Shaw for permission to reproduce the epigraph on p. v.

*Egypt from
Independence to
Revolution,
1919-1952*

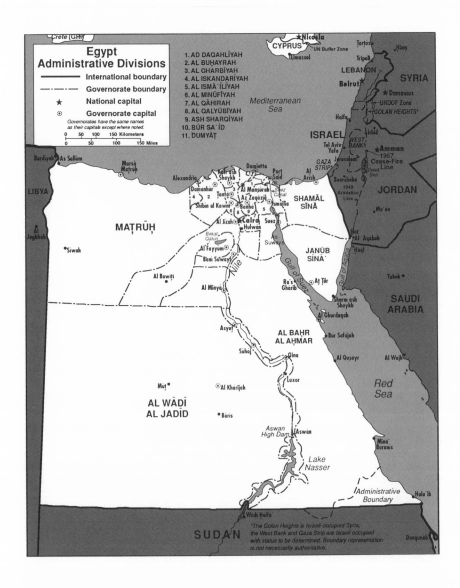

[1]
Introduction

Typically, students of modern Egypt have tended to focus either broadly on the British occupation of the country and the effects of Western influence and penetration or more narrowly on discrete political or economic issues of a particular period. The tendency has been to recount the lives of the more famous Egyptian personalities, people whose creative or intellectual accomplishments, political influence, or business acumen have had a significant and recognizable impact on the society. People and groups outside the mainstream, however, have been less well understood.

This work departs from the more traditional studies on Egypt because it focuses not only on conventional political and social forces but also on the less traditional ones. Its intention is to convey the diversity of political experience in the country and to highlight the important economic and intellectual trends that together characterized Egypt during its so-called liberal era. The period covered concentrates on the years between the 1919 revolution and the 1952 coup d'etat, an era when industrial advances, ideological conflict, nationalist fervor, and war shaped a nation in the process of finding its own direction for development and progress. It was an era during which a form of political pluralism existed and provided an opportunity for political expression, participation, and collective experiences. These years, so active and yet so unsatisfactorily understood, have not been replicated in Egypt since.

The political literature dealing with Egypt's liberal age customarily attributes the rise of liberalism and the practice of pluralism in the country to a small, selective political leadership that had education, at least some degree of wealth and standing, and realistic access to power through its connection to the political center. The argument set forth in this study suggests that although European-style liberalism and pluralism were brought to the country by political elites and as processes were manipulated by them, in fact these trends were also embraced and at times exercised by nonparliamentary, nonmainstream groups that were seeking changes in the basic structures of Egyptian society.

This study not only attempts to describe the existing parliamentary structure, which included occasional elections, assembly meetings, and some discussion of issues, but also hopes to convey the mushrooming activities of people outside the political center, who increasingly intervened in political life to voice their own demands. The conventional accounts of this period generally overlook the nascent, often uncertain, and mostly irregular attempts of the popular classes to participate in the political process. This book, by contrast, assesses political activity at both the elite and nonelite levels. It argues that significant political activity occurred in Egypt, not only through legislative initiative and parliamentary debate, but also as a result of the entrance of the more humble social classes into the political arena through membership in such groups as Young Egypt, the Muslim Brotherhood, and the Communist movement.

If political pluralism thrived during these years, competing ideologies that arose out of the circumstances of the time and captured the sentiments of an eager audience were the cause. The structure for the pluralist system was provided by the liberal democratic framework, but pluralism was actually put into operation and made meaningful by all those Egyptians who participated in politics and communicated their collective will.

Liberal ideology was imported from Europe in the pre–World War I period and applied without substantively adjusting it to the requirements of a colonialzed Egypt. The most important

constitutional revisions that did occur accommodated the mis-
givings of an unconvinced monarchy and gave it disproportionate power. This actually weakened democracy in the country. In
the classic Western democratic models, the constitution was considered an inviolable document and acted as a protection against
individual or group tyranny, safeguarding the system against
procedural abuses. It assured, moreover, that the people would
be sovereign. Liberal democratic systems were underwritten by
constitutional guarantees establishing regularized procedures
for electing representatives to office and maintaining them there
for an allotted period of time. Increasingly, these procedures allowed for the participation of the common person in the political
process and endorsed the idea that the government should re-
spond to the legitimate demands of the majority of the citizenry.

With the promulgation of the Constitution of 1923 in Egypt,
democratic processes and institutions were put into place. The
framers of Egyptian democracy adopted the principle of popular
sovereignty, incorporated political pluralism into the system, endorsed amicable competition between aspirants to office, and
accepted the idea of simplified voting requirements. Political
parties were formed, a relatively free press was sanctioned, a
two-tiered parliament was created, and periodic elections were
to be held whose theoretical purpose was to allow a significant
part of the population to influence policy by choosing political
functionaries to represent it. In the budding liberal democratic
state, however, the Constitution gave excessive powers to the
monarch, who was granted authority to dismiss cabinets, dis-
solve parliaments, and appoint and unseat prime ministers. Because the king often chose his ministers from the small minority
parties, he regularly elevated otherwise unpopular, unelectable,
and undemocratic men to the highest political office. With this
authority, Kings Fuad and Faruq repeatedly demonstrated their
intolerance of liberal democracy and obstructed the constitutional process.

The effort to institutionalize liberal democracy and political pluralism was also weakened by local social and economic conditions. In the West, democracy developed after the birth of a bourgeois class, a class whose interest in opening up the economic system also encouraged the evolution and expansion of the political process. Society in the West had reached a certain level of education and literacy, industrialization, urbanization, and per capita income level.[1] Moreover, individual citizens began participating in voluntary organizations such as trade unions, professional organizations, and religious groups, which raised their level of interest and encouraged an active citizenry. Egypt, between the start of World War I and the close of World War II, had neither a thriving indigenous bourgeoisie nor a large proletariat. Rural life prevailed in Egypt, and social mobility, for most members of the society was unrealistic. The state educational system was primitive, and although industrial growth had taken place, it could not always be sustained or developed. In general, the social, economic, and demographic characteristics of underdevelopment so common in the Middle East and North Africa were likewise present in Egypt. To be sure, these were not inconsiderable handicaps. Moreover, the social indoctrination that originated in the family unit also constrained democratic practice. As both Andrea Rugh and Saad Eddin Ibrahim have separately suggested, the Egyptian family did not help in the creation of a democratic state by providing an infrastructural base. Being highly authoritarian and hierarchical in structure,[2] the family promoted acquiescence rather than defiance, acceptance rather than questioning.[3]

Ultimately, Egypt's liberal experience was both imperfect and impermanent. Egregious transgressions were committed against democracy while it was young and vulnerable: culpable were supposed friends of the process as well as its known enemies. Not only did palace favorites scoff at democratic privileges, but the smaller minority parties (the Wafd's competitors) exerted enormous effort to breach the spirit of constitutionalism in the country. Even the Wafd party, the premier nationalist and liberal organization in Egypt, shifted some of its positions and loyalties over time in attempts to gain power. Unfortunately, the Wafd did not envision its role as a builder of democratic forces; it too was content to operate in a system that had built-in mechanisms for the obstruction of constitutional rights.

Yet, against the odds, in this semiliberal society struggling to find its way politically, ideological pluralism did exist. In addition to secular and more traditionally oriented elected political officials who were philosophically committed to democratic practice, there were militant Islamic fundamentalists, dedicated leftists, evolving feminists, and independent nationalists, who reflected a wide spectrum of political ideas and whose activity suggested a desire to participate in the political process.

The secular nationalist movement was led by the Wafd party. It galvanized the patriotism of much of the popular and upper classes and activated their energies. For much of the liberal period, the Wafd was the hegemonic nationalist party in Egypt. It became the center of an anti-British movement of national unity that stretched throughout Egypt and won supporters from all sectors of the population, from the poor peasant to the big landlord, from urban workers and artisans to intellectuals and merchants. Egyptian nationalists were actively trying to win complete self-determination from the British, who were still exerting political influence even though Egypt had been nominally independent since 1922. During this period, national liberation became a rallying cry for Egyptians from all social classes, age groups, and places of residence. Fighting tenaciously for sovereignty, Egyptians won their rights slowly, first in 1922 with limited independence, later in 1936 and 1954 with the Anglo-Egyptian treaties, and finally in 1956 after total British evacuation. Because of Britain's long-standing presence, Egyptian politics was dominated in this period by the demand for national independence; appeals for social and economic progress were subjugated to an issue of external origin.

Because the Wafd was the most serious political party in the country, its participation was critical in any major debate and in any major negotiation with the British. No mainstream party, no secular leader, could convince the mass of the population to endorse a political change unless the Wafd was involved. But other groups also worked hard to influence the course of political life in the country. During these years, the Muslim Brotherhood, Young Egypt, the Wafdist Vanguard, the Feminist Union, and Communist groups such as the Egyptian Movement for National Liberation, Iskra, and the New Dawn emerged and flourished precisely because the system of politics allowed for a multiplicity of views. It was not aberrational that these groups were able to recruit, organize, hold demonstrations, encourage labor strikes, and print newspapers and leaflets with the intensity they displayed, especially in the 1930s and the 1940s. Rather, it was a testament to the political system in place, faulty, incomplete, and struggling for legitimacy as it was.

Watershed events such as World Wars I and II irrevocably changed Egypt, contributed to social, economic, and political transformation, and made this period a particularly exciting juncture in Egyptian political history. War stimulated industrialization and self-sufficiency and contributed to the growth of new ideas that led to the militancy of a political opposition. The ideological diversity and political and intellectual ferment that most notably characterized the late 1930s and 1940s continued to develop, and not many years later, a group of low-level military officers who were sufficiently alienated and angered by the inability of the existing leadership to address the burning questions of the day plotted the overthrow of the monarchy. As a result of their coup d'etat in 1952, the Free Officers successfully changed the structure of political, economic, and social life in Egypt.

The purpose of this book is to expose readers to general themes and events current in modern Egypt: the role of nationalism in a semicolonized country, the experience of political pluralism in a limited democracy, the impact of war, the birth of new social groups in response to domestic changes, and the influence of culture in a largely illiterate society. It offers background information essential for the understanding of contemporary Egyptian society.

[2]
The Egyptians

Many images come to mind when one thinks of Egypt: the pyramids, the ancient tombs of Luxor, the Nile River, the rich farmlands of the Delta Valley, traditional village life, al-Azhar University, Cairo with its markets, mosques, and minarets, and Alexandria with its beaches on the Mediterranean and its cosmopolitan flair. Equally distinctive and as tenacious are the Egyptian people—those peasants, craftsmen, industrial workers, soothsayers, midwives, street vendors, professionals, students, landowners, and businessmen who make up the population and who, along with sometimes unwelcomed foreigners, have determined the country's movements and rhythms.

Although, for some, Egypt seems unchanged—and unchanging—since time immemorial, the history of Egypt is actually a dynamic one. Timeless customs, informed by religion or ritual, have been transferred from generation to generation, but the country's economic, political, and social structures developed with the passage of years and the practices of rulers. Egyptian society has been deeply affected by its history of foreign domination, but its sense of identity and pride have been maintained through the years, possibly as a result of its long and celebrated history.

Egyptians are, of course, proud of their ancient glories; they look with affection upon the tombs, the treasures, and the monuments produced by their forebears. But in the political and ideological climate of the late 1980s and early 1990s, when this book was written, the majority of Egyptians were expressing deep attachments to their Islamic roots. This work opens, therefore, with a short overview of Egyptian political history beginning with the Islamic period.

Political Life

Up until 639, when Egypt was conquered by the newly constituted Arab armies and became part of the Islamic Empire, it was Byzantine controlled. The Muslim conquerors successfully defeated their opponents, thanks in part to aid from the indigenous population of Coptic Christians. The Copts despised their Byzantine overlords and were hopeful that the Arabs would prove more lenient rulers. Over time, Egypt was Arabized and Islamicized; the Coptic community became a minority of the population, and the Coptic language became liturgical, learned only by a handful of priests.

Arab governors maintained control of the country only until 834. At that time, the Abbasid rulers of the Islamic Empire, who generally governed their dominions through Turkish military and political functionaries, granted Egypt to members of the Turkish oligarchy. One notable Abbasid governor of Turkish origin, Ahmad Ibn Tulun, whose famous mosque still stands in Cairo, was the first in a chain of rulers who established an autonomous state in Egypt. In 969, a new North African dynasty, the Ismaili Fatimids, won control of Egypt and established their capital in Cairo. Egypt was turned from a Sunni Islamic state into one dominated by the Shi'i Islamic sect and remained so for two centuries.

When Salah al-Din put an end to the Fatimid dynasty in 1171, he reestablished Sunni orthodoxy, which is still practiced in Egypt today. Salah al-Din's descendants governed Egypt until 1250.

From 1250 until 1517, Egypt was ruled by a military dynasty of white slaves of Turkic origin called mamluks. Originally bought by Turks as young boys in the Russian Urals, the Central Asian

1. Entrance to the Great Pyramid

steppes, or the Caucasus Mountains, the mamluk youth were trained as soldiers, instructed in Arabic, and converted to Islam. They were organized in households and were fiercely loyal to those who brought them up. Even after they were freed from slavery at the age of puberty, their allegiances were focused upon the brotherhood that had trained them, disciplined them, and introduced them to their world of warfare and domination. As a result of their governmental and military skills, the mamluks gained and maintained control of Egypt for more than two hundred and fifty years.

In 1517, the Ottomans defeated the mamluks, and Egypt became one of the subject Arab provinces of the large and heterogeneous Ottoman Empire. The mamluks, who had been enrolled in the Ottoman military corps and had become governors and high military officers, retained a dominant position in the administration; but the Ottomans were able to impose their will upon them whenever they wished. Indeed, by the sixteenth and seventeenth centuries, the Ottomans had built a world empire predicated on a disciplined military and superior arms. But their supremacy did not continue into the industrial era. When the Ottomans subsequently began to lose their strength to the rising European powers, Ottoman commerce, culture, science, and even military methods were affected. By the time Napoleon landed in Egypt in 1798 with a substantial military force and a retinue of scientists and orientalists, the country had already become linked to, and influenced by, economic movements and political trends in Europe. Napoleon's expedition was one concrete indication that nations on the European continent were on the move and looking aggressively toward the Middle East to expand their economic and strategic relations. Although Napoleon had the ambitious goal of colonizing Egypt for the French, his occupation lasted only three short years.

After the French were compelled by an Ottoman-English force to leave Egypt, a political vacuum existed. While the Ottomans, the mamluks, and the British forces were competing to elevate

2. Full view of the Sphinx

their particular candidate to the position of governor of Egypt, a little-known Albanian mercenary who had come to the country as part of the Ottoman army gained control of the situation. Muhammad Ali, who later became known as the "father of modern Egypt," built an alliance with the religious establishment, the *ulema*, and was able to play one contender against another, eliminate his rivals, and become governor in 1805. Thus once again Egypt was ruled by a foreigner, another Turkic speaker. Members of the Muhammad Ali dynasty were responsible for much development and modernization in Egypt. They presided over the country until 1952, when Gamal Abdul Nasser, a native Egyptian, overthrew the government and ousted King Faruq, the last member of the Muhammad Ali family to head the country.

Muhammad Ali Pasha directed a state-based economy with agricultural, industrial, and commercial sectors. He oversaw the production of the valuable long-staple cotton crop, which became the mainstay of the economic system. By abolishing the traditional system of tax farming, which had decentralized agriculture, and by becoming the sole landowner, he established control over the soil and its resources, and over the people and their labors. He built new industrial establishments and stood at the helm of a modernized military that used new weapons and European-style uniforms and training. Eager to expand his area of control, he led his troops in military campaigns in Syria, Sudan, and Arabia.

Muhammad Ali's dream was to build a modern and prosperous country, ruled dynastically by members of his family. He was a stern leader with considerable ambition and great vision, but he was not popular. In order to transform Egypt in the way he envisaged, he disrupted village life and the pattern of agricultural work; he weakened the guild system by encouraging state intervention in economic affairs and by opening Egypt up to foreign goods; and he accelerated the breakdown of tribal life by enticing chiefs into government positions. Muhammad Ali provoked controversy because he conscripted peasants into the military, forced women into the labor force, and monopolized the state and the economy.[1]

The Ottomans feared that Muhammad Ali's domestic ambitions and his irridentist intentions threatened their official control over Egypt and the region. In reaction, they joined in alliance with similarly anxious Europeans and forced Muhammad Ali to give up his system of monopolies, pull back his troops from outside Egypt, and acknowledge the central government in Constantinople. The Ottomans and the Europeans checked Muhammad Ali's power before it grew uncontrollable; they weakened him as a ruler and undermined his plans for development.

Of all Muhammad Ali's successors, his grandson Ismail had perhaps the most dramatic impact on the country. With political interests both inside Egypt and abroad, he hoped to convert his country into a European-like nation independent of the Ottomans. He looked forward to a time when Egypt would be a model of development and a showpiece of creativity. Coming to power in 1863, at a time of economic prosperity in Egypt, Ismail (now formally called the Khedive) improved canals, bridges, and telegraph lines; he extended the railway system, expanded the ports, and bettered the postal services. Along with this, he reformed the educational system by establishing specialized schools for lawyers, administrators, engineers, teachers, and technicians; he also encouraged the education of girls. In 1869, he presided over the opening of the Suez Canal, the culmination of a project that had begun ten years earlier, with a lavish and extravagant party that brought the leaders of European society and politics to Egypt.

As a way of strengthening his economic base, Ismail brought more land under cultivation for the cotton crop. But he learned all too painfully that since cotton was a highly fluctuating product in the world marketplace, he could not depend on it as a reliable source of revenue to fund his ambitious program of modernization. By 1875, the resources of the state had been stretched

3. Upper-Egyptian village women

to their limit, and a financial crisis could not be avoided. When the economy faltered, Ismail sought financial help from the European powers he was trying so hard to imitate. He also sold his own shares in the Suez Canal Company, amounting to 44 percent of the total; but he was still unable to overcome his financial difficulties.

A year later, when Egypt was incapable of meeting its financial responsibilities to its European creditors, an international debt commission was established. In essence, France and Britain began to control Egypt's economy. They showed little regard for local concerns and were mainly interested in satisfying Egypt's creditors; as a result, Egypt in the late 1870s and early 1880s was plagued by economic insolvency and political instability. As a result of the deteriorating conditions in his country, Ismail was forced to abdicate his position. In response, a military officer and Egyptian patriot, Ahmad Urabi, led an antigovernment, antiforeign revolt, directing his protest against both the Turkish pashas, who controlled most civil, military, and social posts of importance, and the Europeans, whose vision of Egypt conflicted with his own. Although he managed to excite and engage sections of the populace and set something of a precedent for nationalist upheaval, his actions ultimately contributed to the British occupation of Egypt. In 1882, Britain intervened to control the nascent nationalist movement and eliminate what it deemed to be the potentially destructive political confusion that had emerged in Egypt.

Great Britain occupied Egypt for both financial and strategic reasons, gaining a decisive voice in all areas of Egyptian life: agriculture, commerce, education, health, welfare, the military, and the economy. Throughout the occupation (which lasted until 1956 in various forms), technological, agricultural, and industrial growth was slow, never keeping pace with the rise in population. Conscious of the privileges and superior material conditions of Europeans resident in the country, Egyptians bitterly resented foreign domination. In reaction, a vibrant nationalist movement emerged that at times marshaled the support of virtually the entire populace in demonstrations and protests against British authority. The struggle for national self-determination was embraced by people across the political spectrum, from those on the revolutionary left to those on the Islamic right, with many moderates in between. Egyptians firmly believed that they had an incontrovertible right to exist as a nation. Confident that they could manage their own affairs, make the appropriate political decisions, and administer the laws they chose to enact, Egyptians wholeheartedly endorsed the nationalist campaign.

By the time Egypt received its first liberal constitution in 1923, the Egyptian population had already endured an international conflict (World War I) and a national upheaval (the Egyptian revolution of 1919). Moreover, as the era of liberalism commenced, Egyptians were becoming increasingly involved in political activity. In contrast to the conventional view that the Egyptian masses have consistently adopted an apathetic posture toward the political process, this book will argue that Egyptians participated in a variety of political activities during the first half of the twentieth century. They consistently raised their voices at moments of national crisis and called for change; they periodically demonstrated and protested in the streets despite intimidation and possible repression; they even joined nonmainstream political organizations such as the Muslim Brotherhood, Young Egypt, and parties of the underground revolutionary left. In addition, whenever given the opportunity, Egyptians expressed their political preferences through the mechanism of elections, casting votes in particular, and enthusiastically, for the Wafd party, which was founded following World War I as a mass nationalist organization. The activism of the population was not encouraged by the political establishment per se. Rather, it was self-generated and ironically often inspired concern on the part of elected officials, who wanted to control the political sentiments of the masses, not unleash them.

In fact, owing to the limited constitutionalism and imperfect democratic procedures of the pre-Nasser period, Egyptians often found themselves intentionally cut off from governmental authority and mainstream sources of power. Decision making was deliberately accomplished at the highest levels of society without consulting the people and with minimal negotiation among disparate groups. Essentially, a handful of powerful individuals whose prominence was due to social status, economic advantage, or leadership ambition almost singlehandedly ran the country and controlled the population. Not even the Wafd party, despite its liberal appearance and self-proclaimed commitment to constitutionalism, entertained the notion of fundamentally altering the structure of political practice. Though it did make party politics both attractive and at times useful to the common man and woman, and though it did give citizens their first real vehicle through which to voice nationalist grievances lawfully, the Wafd was not inclined to weaken the tradition of elite-based politics in the country.

As a result, a prevailing feature of political life in Egypt throughout the twentieth century has been strong individual authority. One reason for this was that Egypt's antidemocratic monarchs felt challenged by constitutionalism and encouraged, whenever possible, rule by the individual. In addition, however, celebrated political figures such as Saad Zaghlul, Ismail Sidqi, and Mustafa al-Nahhas perpetuated the system of personality politics in the country by dominating political life. And when the 1952 revolution brought a new generation of leaders to power, they too demanded absolute control. As a result, nontraditional and especially lower-class political forces have been detached from the political mainstream and excluded from access to power.

Social Life

For centuries, Egypt has been a rigidly stratified society, with a few rich and powerful families at the top and the mass of the population, impoverished and cut off from political power, below. The propertied classes have always constituted a relatively small number of people, but because they have been dominant in virtually every sphere of life, their impact has been disproportionate. Upper-echelon society intersected on many levels: in business, in politics, in social relations, and in marriage. Exclusivity meant that well-to-do families typically lived in particular areas, educated their children in separate schools, and engaged only in certain occupational fields.

In the twentieth century, Egypt was a land of extremes. In contrast to the peasants who lived along the ribbon of the Nile and the urban proletariat crowded into poor neighborhoods in Cairo, Alexandria, and their environs, there were rich landlords, aristocrats, businessmen, and government officials who lived a European-style life of culture and sophistication. Except where the rich were personally served by the poor, rarely did the two worlds converge.

Egypt remained an agricultural country until after World War II. Agriculture provided sustenance to Egypt's inhabitants in spite of the country's rugged desert topography, which drastically limited the area of land available for cultivation. The Nile River irrigated and fertilized Egypt's land, provided its material security, and contributed to the rituals, celebrations, and traditions of the population. Its waters allowed for the growth of long-staple cotton, the most important cash crop grown for export since the 1820s. Considered among the best strains of cotton in the world and grown successfully as a result of Egypt's soil and climate, the crop provided Egypt with necessary foreign exchange. Exclusive reliance on cotton had, however, ultimately detrimental consequences. It inhibited the local production of foodstuffs necessary to feed the growing population and left the economy dependent on a single crop whose value fluctuated widely on the international market.

In the first half of the twentieth century, Egyptian agriculture was extremely backward. Typically, peasants used the same style of equipment and the same methods as their ancestors had for centuries before them. Landownership was characteristically uneven; most property belonged to absentee landlords living comfortably in the city, who felt little concern for their peasants. Land was rented to tenants, and the rent was paid either in cash or in kind. The landlord controlled the allocation of water, the system of drainage, and the schedule of crop rotations. Leases were generally short-term, rarely exceeding two or three years. Landowners had little impetus to technologize their farms: labor was cheap, and peasants, who were historically skeptical of change, would likely have resisted innovation if it had been proposed.

Population growth, land parcelization, and gradual but increasing industrialization led to growing urbanization during the first half of the twentieth century. Egypt's population rose rapidly during this period. In 1917, it was about 12,670,000, of whom about 790,000 were in Cairo. By 1947, the population had reached 18,806,000, with over 2,000,000 in Cairo, which had grown at over three times the rate of Egypt as a whole.

Industrial development reacted to key changes in the economic and political situations and accelerated during particular periods: during World Wars I and II as a result of civilian shortages and military requirements, and during the 1930s after the 1930 tariff laws protected local industry against foreign imports. In particular, Egyptian factories produced textiles, foodstuffs, and chemicals, supplying some of the needs of the local population. But industry in this impoverished country suffered from the adverse conditions found in most underdeveloped Third World countries: the narrowness of the home market, the absence of local fuels and cheap electrical power, the lack of technicians and skilled workers, the absence of an entrepreneurial spirit among the moneyed classes; and the reluctance of the government to assist investors by passing appropriate legislation.[2]

Although the economic life of Egypt was changing, the everyday world of the Egyptian, be he or she peasant, villager, or

4. Village life

urban dweller, was relatively constant. Struggling to provide for
a family's well-being, the typical head of household earned only
a very small income and provided at best humble accommoda-
tions and a simple diet of bread, cheese, beans, onions, sugar,
and some fruit. Furthermore, poor health was a constant for the
indigent: trachoma, tuberculosis, dysentery, and malaria were
ever-present maladies, and parasitic diseases such as bilharziasis
and ankylostoma were endemic, sapping the strength and ex-
hausting the energies of the population. In contrast, for the more
affluent sections of society, the quality of life was superior. These

Egyptians ate meat, vegetables, rice, and wheat, lived in better quarters, were cared for by qualified health professionals, and enjoyed the cultural life the urban centers offered.

In this period, the Egyptian population was overwhelmingly Muslim, but a Coptic minority survived, numbering perhaps one and a half million people in the 1940s. Up until the 1950s, small but thriving cosmopolitan communities of nonethnic Egyptians also existed. Notably of Jewish, Armenian, Greek, and Italian origin, many had been born in Egypt but were unassimilated into the mass culture. Generally, they had access to better schools and more attractive employment, serving as businessmen, teachers, translators, technicians, shopkeepers, and skilled workers.

Throughout the early twentieth century, there was an effort to Egyptianize the country and to raise the indigenous population to the level of the Europeans, or at least to the level of the Europeanized Egyptians resident there. Simultaneously, there was a constant demand that Egyptians take over the administration of Egypt. These appeals were directed at Britain, the occupying power, and at Britain's clients in Egypt, and eventually they were heard and addressed. The first stirrings of change were felt in 1936, when the Anglo-Egyptian Treaty allotted more local power to the Egyptians. Later, the nationalist activity from the mid-1940s onward, the effects of the Palestine War of 1948, and the revolution of 1952 itself gave increasing immediacy to the movement of Egyptianization. When Abdul Nasser staged his coup and took over the presidency, native Egyptians decisively gained control of their country for the first time in centuries. No longer were the money-makers, the moneylenders, the journalists, the jewelry makers, the department store owners, and the machinists of predominantly European ethnic origin. Now most were of indigenous stock, as were the technocrats, the military officers, and the high officials. After Nasser's accession, the status of the minority population had to change as many people left Egypt or took on more secondary roles in business and the professions. A new phase of Egyptian history had begun.

[3]
Occupation and the Nationalist Response

The Quest for Independence

When Great Britain occupied Egypt in 1882, the country was legally part of the Ottoman Empire. After the Ottomans sided with the Germans in 1914, the British government severed Egypt's ceremonial connection with the Turks and declared the country a British protectorate, changing its territorial status and regularizing Anglo control. Even though many Egyptians of political stature expected the protectorate to be a temporary arrangement limited to the duration of the war, they were still dissatisfied. Egyptians from all walks of life wanted their full and legitimate nationalist aspirations to be respected.

As World War I progressed, the British became more aggressive in their efforts to control the entire country. In addition to British civil servants who were brought to Cairo to run the bureaucracy, British Empire troops swarmed the larger cities. With the war came high inflation and a degree of hardship that was painful to the majority of the population. In consequence, Anglo-Egyptian hostility deepened, with each side locking into a nonnegotiable position. Egypt demanded unconditional national independence; Britain refused, citing the need to protect its own strategic alliance by keeping Egypt part of the imperial system. The Egyptians became deeply resentful of the British presence, and the occupation was an unpopular one.

Conflict often serves as a catalyst for militancy, and World War I was no exception. In Egypt, a political culture was forming in reaction to two simultaneous and interacting factors. First, the nationalist struggle revived and intensified as issues were brought more clearly into focus and activists were given renewed momentum. Quite simply, years of dictatorship under the British leadership of Lord Cromer and Herbert Kitchener motivated the nationalists to demand immediate change. Second, the war affected the Egyptian population in material ways. Numbers of Egyptians were conscripted into the war effort and suffered deprivation, and the civilian population as well endured high prices and food shortages. In the countryside, for example, military authorities forced the peasants to exchange grain, cotton, and livestock for limited compensation. Throughout Egypt, hoarders and war profiteers took advantage of the war and made substantial gains despite the misery of the larger population.

In addition, the British authorities imposed restrictive measures, such as media censorship and martial law, designed to curb the population's movements and principally to keep its nationalist militants, active since the start of the occupation, under the authorities' watchful eyes. Ultimately, this proved impossible. By the close of the conflict the nationalist leader, Saad Zaghlul, with support from the entire country, openly demanded that Egyptians be allowed to determine their own destiny. In particular, Zaghlul asked that he be allowed to head an Egyptian delegation (in Arabic, *wafd*) that would travel to the Paris Peace Conference and be empowered to put forward the nationalist claim for independence. Despite the fact that Reginald Wingate, the British high commissioner resident in Egypt, thought that the British should talk to Zaghlul and allow him to plead his nation's case, London refused. In London's view, Zaghlul had no official status, and although he had served as minister of education and minister of justice, he was not considered well enough placed to warrant international attention.

Despite British attempts to dissuade them, the Egyptians pro-

ceeded with their plans. In November 1918, an Egyptian delegation of nationalist politicians and well-placed notables was
formed and prepared itself to represent Egypt at the postwar
conference in Paris. This became the nucleus of the famed Wafd
party led by Saad Zaghlul, a towering figure who is regarded as
one of the greatest nationalist heroes in Egypt's modern history.
Zaghlul's passionate defense of Egyptian independence inspired
otherwise quiescent crowds to participate in the political culture,
support the nationalist campaign, and engage in militant activity
against the British occupation.

Revered as the archetypal patriot in Egypt even today, Zaghlul
is remembered for his activities, his speeches, and his commitment to national independence. Who was Saad Zaghlul, and
why is his legacy so notable? The son of a moderately wealthy
village headman, Zaghlul studied at mosque schools and at al-
Azhar where he was influenced by the great Muslim reformers
Jamal al-Din al-Afghani and Muhammad Abduh. His nationalist
activity dated back to the early 1880s, when Ahmad Urabi led an
antigovernment, antiforeign revolt in an attempt to give Egyptians control over their political and economic affairs. Soon after
the British occupied Egypt, Zaghlul went to France to study.
When he returned to Egypt, he first practiced law, then became
a judge in the national court system, and later minister of education (1906) and minister of justice (1910). In January 1914, Zaghlul
was elected to the short-lived Legislative Assembly, where he
became a leading opponent of the occupation.[1]

Early in his life, Zaghlul determined that moderation would
not lead the nationalists to victory. The British, he believed, were
already too committed to incorporating Egypt into their empire
and to exploiting the diplomatic and strategic advantages that
had been won. Zaghlul's eloquence and his heart-felt, uncompromising attitude encouraged activism in the country. In 1919,
he harnessed already widespread anti-British sentiment into a
nationalist movement of significance that demanded a British
withdrawal from the Nile Valley. In consequence, Zaghlul was

speedily arrested by British military personnel on March 8 of that year, along with others from his circle, including Ismail Sidqi and Muhammad Mahmud, and deported to Malta. Within days, the country erupted in revolt, protesting against the deportation of Zaghlul, the British occupation, and Britain's refusal to allow Egyptian nationalists to represent their country in negotiations to determine Egypt's postwar status. Students, government employees, workers, lawyers, and professionals took to the streets, demonstrating, protesting, and proclaiming that the Wafd was their legitimate representative. Throughout the country, British installations were attacked, railway lines damaged, and the nationalist movement gained credibility with Zaghlul being confirmed as its undisputed leader.

What originated as a peaceful political proposal initiated by largely upper-class Egyptian notables, who were influenced by the speeches of President Woodrow Wilson of the United States defending national self-determination, turned into revolutionary activity carried out by the mass of the population. Ironically, the intention of the Wafd was not to spearhead political revolution nor stimulate social change but to activate highly placed Egyptians and, through concerted peaceful activity from above, convince the British to surrender power. As the situation crystallized, however, the population became more radicalized than the party itself. Like people in other colonized countries throughout the world in the postwar period, Egyptians found that their desire for national self-determination intensified and provided the basis of the protest.

The revolution did not evict the British from the Nile Valley, but it did politicize a population that had rediscovered national pride and gained a measure of power in nationalist politics. This forced a reluctant General Edmund Allenby, the new high commissioner, and the British government to acknowledge Zaghlul as an appropriate person with whom to negotiate and to recall him from exile. In April, Zaghlul and his associates were freed. Believing themselves to be the legitimate representatives of

Egypt's nationalist movement, they then proceeded to the postwar peace conference with high hopes for Egyptian independence backed up by the recent events that unmistakably demonstrated the depths of popular support for independence. They believed in Egypt as a nation, legitimately incorporating Muslims, Copts, and other minorities into an explicitly secular nation.[2] Although confident that the nationalist movement had won an important first victory, their expectations were short-lived. On the same day that the delegation arrived in Paris, the American envoys recognized Britain's protectorate over Egypt.[3] Since Egypt's right to self-rule was not established, the delegation came home sorely disappointed.

Between 1919 and 1922, attempts to negotiate for an independent constitutional monarchy failed to produce results. The British were simply not yet prepared to come to terms with an autonomous Egyptian leadership, nor eager to give away their hold on such a strategically located country. They would have liked to find a pro-British group willing to conclude a treaty that safeguarded British and foreign interests in the country. But they were unable to do so. Meanwhile, Zaghlul's persistent nationalist activity and his stubborn defense of Egypt's right to self-determination kept the matter alive for the whole population. This led to his second arrest and another term in exile in the Seychelles Islands in the Indian Ocean.

Grudgingly, after three years of unfruitful exchanges, the British came to the recognition that an Anglo-Egyptian treaty that only preserved the status quo could not be negotiated. In consequence, the British decided unilaterally in 1922 to allow Egypt formal independence. Sovereignty was granted, above all, because of the realistic possibility that the 1919 revolution could recur. This revolution had generated the declaration of independence and given form to the emerging political culture in Egypt, a culture influenced by what Israel Gershoni and James Jankowski call the "territorially defined nation-state."[4]

The proclamation of independence, however, did not prove to

be a panacea. It was limited by four British-imposed conditions: the security of communications for the British Empire, the defense of Egypt against foreign aggression, the protection of foreign interests and minorities, and the British administration of the Sudan. The British defended their own strategic interests and allowed those residents with foreign passports to retain the status and privileges granted to them either by the occupation or by the system of Capitulations[5] centuries earlier. The provisions that sanctioned the privileges of non-Egyptians were particularly displeasing. Egypt of the pre-Nasser period was dominated by foreigners: the British controlled the upper levels of the military and the government, and people of various European nationalities owned and operated the banks, hotels, textile factories, and insurance companies. In 1922, the Egyptians had gained only partial independence.

Along with the announcement of independence came the declaration of the Constitution in 1923, establishing the two-chamber Parliament with its Senate and Chamber of Deputies elected by male suffrage, except for the two-fifths of the Senate who were appointed by the king. (The British also changed the title of Egypt's head of state from sultan to king.) The Constitution stipulated that legislative authority was to be shared by the king, the Senate, and the Chamber of Deputies. Bills enacted by the Parliament did not acquire the status of law until signed by the monarch. If the king rejected a piece of legislation and sent it back to the ministers for amendment, they in turn could pass the original bill with a two-thirds majority; the king was then obliged to sign it into law.[6]

Though patterned on a Belgian model, the Egyptian Constitution was written by Egyptian legal experts who were sympathetic to the king and the British. Their intention, made possible through the legal document, was to limit the strength of the Wafd and to constrain the mass popular movement that had emerged during the 1919 revolution. Despite Wafdist objections to provisions within the Constitution and a bitter political struggle, the Constitution was nevertheless promulgated.[7]

Despite deep dissatisfaction with the restrictions on sovereignty, most Egyptians accepted the Constitution and their limited independence and turned their attention to creating workable institutions through which they could administer their country. Regrettably, however, for the youthful democratic state, the framers of the Constitution gave excessive powers to the monarch, who was granted authority to remove cabinets, suspend Parliament, and install or dismiss prime ministers. During the next thirty years, Kings Fuad and Faruq found many ways to subvert the constitutional process and oppose the nationalist movement.

In contrast, the Wafd party developed into a tenacious political organization that, at least for its first two decades, defended the Constitution as the sole guarantee against antidemocratic behavior. The Wafd saw itself, and was seen by others, as the image of liberal democracy in Egypt that represented a new Egyptian political elite distinct from the Turkish-Circassian origins of previous leaders. Wafdist leaders were indigenous Egyptians who came from the rural landed middle class as well as from the commercial and professional urban elites. The party claimed to represent people of all social classes and from all geographical areas. It attracted both Muslims and Copts into its ranks, which was seen as a considerable accomplishment.

The Wafd's popularity was nationally recognized, but the party's ability to win elections and its vocal support for the system of liberal democracy did not assure it the opportunity to head successive governments. Given the slightest provocation, the king invoked constitutional privilege and disallowed the Wafd from taking power, deliberately confining the party to minority political status. In consequence, although Egypt exhibited the forms of Western-style constitutionalism, its practice was seriously flawed because of the infractions upon the Constitution perpetrated by the palace and its appointed ministers. Although designed as a semiliberal political entity, the Constitution could not fully sustain liberalism's democratic content. Despite a multiplicity of political parties, elections, parliamentary sessions, and differing degrees of freedom of the press and association, the Constitution was infrequently applied and limited in effect. Democratic practice thus was periodically paralyzed. In this context, neither the Wafd nor any other political organization successfully exercised a brake on the absolutism of the king.

In essence, consistent democratic practice was absent in Egypt because no truly mass political party was capable of pressuring the king to relax his hold on the political arena. Arguably, only a system that encouraged mass participation and responded to the demands of the majority of the population could have compelled both the monarch and the ironfisted political elites to respect the constitutional laws of the land. Leonard Binder, who has written extensively about Egypt, convincingly argues that the Wafd in the 1920s and 1930s could have acted as a mobilizer of the masses and aggressively brought more people into the political process by expanding its own membership, allowing nonelites to influence policy in the party, and embracing issues of social and economic reform. Wafdist leaders, however, chose not to activate peasants, workers, and members of the lower middle class, preferring instead to recruit and then satisfy the more upper-class constituents. The party leaders did this by focusing almost exclusively on the national question, doing little to expand the democratic system and involve the traditionally disenfranchised in the political arena.[8]

For the Wafd, nationalism was the single most important issue. The nation, as the Wafd defined it, was a combination of groups whose main purpose was to struggle for and then maintain independence.[9] The party was not ideologically suited to address radical social causes and for most of the liberal period simply chose not to fight for social change, fearful of creating a movement it would be unable to control.

The Wafd recognized the advantages of manipulating the popular classes: they were dependable as a striking force in the Wafdist demonstrations, and they were reliable as Wafdist supporters in national elections. But this form of political activity was

5. Cairo street scene

generated by the Wafd for Wafdist purposes and was sporadic and limited at best. The Wafd wanted to restrict the degree to which the masses were politicized and to determine the direction, the intensity, and the character of mass involvement. Wafdist officials were not in favor of political action independent of their leadership, perhaps because they feared that the people may have acted according to their own interests, not according to the principles dictated by the Wafd. Thus, despite being at its peak of popularity in the 1920s and early 1930s and fully aware of the absence of meaningful and sustained political participation, the Wafd did little to encourage activism. As a result of Wafdist restraints on the political process, the masses' connection to mainstream political life in Egypt remained weak. This explains, to some extent at least, why nonparliamentary parties such as the Muslim Brotherhood and Young Egypt were successful in their attempts to engage people and bring them into the political arena.

During this so-called liberal age, four groups alternately wielded power in the country: the palace, the British, the Wafd, and the minority parties, in particular the Liberal Constitutionalist party, the Saadist party, the People's party (al-Shaab), and the Unity party (Ittihad). In contrast to the Wafd, which at times could count on the support of the entire nation at polling stations and at protests and marches, the minority groups were little more than the expression of the personalities who monopolized and manipulated them. Like the Wafd, however, these groups made few attempts when in power to legislatively improve the conditions of the underprivileged. No party in Egypt made issues of social and economic reform essential parts of their platforms. Instead, they subjugated national development to the least common denominator of Egyptian political life: the demand for national liberation. For parliamentary leaders, the Egyptian political arena was dominated by the national question, partly because of Britain's stubborn presence in Egypt and partly because of the traditional ideologies the parties separately represented.

Despite constitutional stipulations, from the close of World War I until the Free Officers' accession in 1952, the struggle for political preeminence was often fought in an antidemocratic fashion. A typical pattern emerged in Egyptian politics: whenever a free election was held, the Wafd would be guaranteed a sweeping victory, but a conflict with the British or the palace would inevitably lead to the resignation or dismissal of the Wafd, the dissolution of Parliament, and the suspension or modification of the Constitution. The Wafd was then forced to remain in opposition until a disagreement between the palace and a minority party, or a decision by the British, caused the Wafd's return to power.

The Experience of Semi-Independence

The Wafd party with Saad Zaghlul won an overwhelming victory in the first Egyptian elections held in 1923. After Zaghlul was appointed prime minister, he presided over sophisticated parliamentary debates and initiated legislative activity, giving hope and reassurance to those who were eager for democracy to take hold. Then an event occurred that touched off a major political crisis in the country and threw the new democratic system into disarray. Sir Lee Stack, the British commander in chief of the Egyptian army and governor of Sudan, was assassinated in 1924 by a disgruntled nationalist group associated with a former Wafdist. The British high commissioner in Egypt, Edmund Allenby, was so angered by the incident that he acted impulsively without first obtaining proper authorization from the government in London. He issued a series of harsh punishments against the Egyptians, the most important being the withdrawal of the Egyptian army from the Sudan, payment of a half million pounds indemnity, and a prohibition against political demonstrations. Allenby's attribution of the crime to Zaghlul, who according to sources knew nothing about it, and the latter's refusal to accept Allenby's ultimatums (with the exception of payment of the indemnity) led to Zaghlul's resignation and also marked the end of his political career, for after his resignation he was never again allowed to serve as prime minister of Egypt.

This assassination proved significant because of the tenor of Allenby's reaction and because of the character of the regime that followed. As though Egypt were still a British protectorate, the high commissioner intervened in Egyptian affairs without regard for the country's new sovereign status and forced Zaghlul's resignation. Allenby simply ignored the new democratic structure in place in Egypt and initiated the process of interventionism that was practiced until Nasser took charge in 1952. In addition, Allenby ensured that the next prime minister, Ahmad Ziwar Pasha, would weaken the Wafd by promoting antidemocratic legislation. In particular, Ziwar amended the electoral laws so that multistage rather than direct elections would take place, gerrymandered districts, wanted the voting age increased, and hoped to impose educational and property requirements on the voters. The intent, of course, was to weaken the democrats. So early into the life of this young semiliberal nation, the rule of democracy was tested. Unfortunately, the young nation was not yet ready to meet the challenge of an aggressive former coloniz- er, an unsympathetic king, and a group of undemocratic politi- cians. As a result, only a year after the Wafdist victory occurred, the hopes of Egyptian democrats were dashed, and the pattern of interventionist, nondemocratic politics was set.

Evidently, the monarchy feared the potentially mushrooming strength of the democrats, for in 1925 when the Wafd again won a majority of seats in Parliament, the king dismissed the chamber nine hours after it had assembled and reappointed his ally Ahmad Ziwar to office. In protest against the blatantly anti- democratic behavior of the monarch, the Liberal Constitutional- ist party—once an early ally of the king—left the government. The king, however, was not without political allies. Shortly after the 1925 election, the Ittihad (Unity) party had been created to give the king the personnel he needed to maintain his control. Joining the new political organization were high-ranking army officers, government functionaries, notables, and monarchists.[10]

The pattern of antidemocratic behavior was again repeated in 1926, when the Wafd won an electoral victory after democratic life was temporarily allowed to resume. This time, the national- ists were frustrated because the British prevented Zaghlul from taking power. Dejected, Zaghlul died soon after in 1927 at the age of sixty-seven. Thereupon, Zaghlul was acclaimed as an ex- emplary leader of the nationalist movement. His statesmanship was admired by both his supporters and his adversaries, and his reputation set a high standard for political activism and commit- ment to principle. However, in his determination to win national independence, he introduced a system of patronage into public life and used violence and public demonstrations as weapons against the opposition.[11] He was domineering in style and personality and confirmed a pattern of absolutist control over party politics that has become a hallmark of Egyptian political life.

Egypt has suffered the consequences of restricted democratic practices since the days of Zaghlul. Zealous politicians, overbearing monarchs, and the interference-prone British adulterated democratic political life and prevented constitutionalism from fully developing. Even Muhammad Mahmud of the Liberal Constitutionalist party dissolved Parliament in 1928 and initiated a period of dictatorial rule that, though punctuated by a Wafdist victory in 1929 and the temporary elevation of Mustafa al-Nahhas to the prime ministry, culminated in the appointment of Ismail Sidqi to office only months later. The constitutional system was thus continually challenged and ultimately rendered meaningless by autocratic politicians who ruled according to their own arbitrary standards.

The 1929 election typifies the relationship between the king and the Wafd party and demonstrates the frailty of the democratic process in Egypt. In this election, the Wafd gained its largest majority to date. Winning 60 percent of the popular vote and 93 percent of the seats, the Wafd with al-Nahhas should have been able to bring about change in the country. The party hoped to negotiate a new treaty with the British, as well as to reestablish the legitimacy of the Constitution in response to opponents' efforts to subvert it.[12] Al-Nahhas had no success with the British, who at this juncture were not inclined to alter the existing status of the country, but perhaps more devastating, he was forced to leave office in disgrace after clashing with the king. Because al-Nahhas was implicated in an alleged corruption scandal (although later exonerated) in which he and two associates were accused of peddling their influence in government to a high bidder, the Wafd lost its opportunity to govern.

The late 1920s and early 1930s constituted a bleak period for constitutionalism in Egypt. Muhammad Mahmud acted arbitrarily with regard to domestic politics and was no more able than Ahmad Ziwar to renegotiate a treaty with the British. After Ismail Sidqi assumed the premiership in 1930, he dissolved Parliament, deferred elections, abolished the Constitution of 1923, and created a new one that gave more authority to the king. Sidqi ruled Egypt through unbridled dictatorship in what is remembered as one of the harshest periods in Egypt's modern political history. Sidqi's intention was to rule without intercession from the Wafd, which he did until 1933 when he resigned after a disagreement with the king. Sidqi was succeeded by Abd al-Fattah Yahya Pasha who ruled in a similarly authoritarian manner until November 1934. Tawfiq Nasim Pasha, a moderate politician sympathetic to the Wafd then temporarily took over as prime minister, and in 1935, a national front of the major political parties demanded the reinstatement of the Constitution of 1923. Finally, the king consented to reestablish the original document.

During the first twelve years of Egypt's constitutional life, few issues existed on which all of the country's major politicians, regardless of orientation, could agree. The one exception was the process of negotiation with the British. Egyptians demanded the end of the occupation, the cancellation of restrictions on the strength of the Egyptian army, the transfer of the army's command from British to Egyptian hands, full authority over the Sudan, and the institution of Egyptian control over its minorities. However, Anglo-Egyptian negotiation efforts failed in 1924, 1927, and 1929–1930. Only as a result of an international crisis, the Italian invasion of Ethiopia in 1936, did Britain soften its position and become amenable to compromise. For the British, fascist Italy, which was now in control of both Libya and Ethiopia, had become a threat and a challenge in the region. The British intention was to keep the Egyptians on the side of the European democracies and averse to fascist ideology and expansionism. This was particularly pressing and fateful since King Fuad and his entourage were suspected of pro-Italian sympathies. In contrast, at least early in the conflict, the majority of Egyptians were skeptical of the fascists and feared that they would be harsher overlords than the British. London recognized that this was an auspicious time to solidify local anti-Mussolini sentiment and thus granted the Egyptians increased autonomy in 1936.

Indeed, 1936 proved to be a year of many changes. Free elections were held, and the Wafd was elected to power. A multiparty delegation, made up of representatives from all of the political parties except the Nationalist party of Mustafa Kamil, was charged with negotiating a settlement with Britain. On August 26, 1936, a historic agreement was reached, and the Anglo-Egyptian Treaty was signed. All of the participants believed the agreement to be advantageous because it moved Egypt further toward independence. The treaty did recognize Egypt as an independent and sovereign nation but also stipulated that Britain would aid Egypt in an emergency, and that Egypt must grant Britain the military facilities required to protect British lines of communication. In essence, this was a defense pact that provided that all of Britain's ten thousand troops were to be limited to the Suez Canal Zone during peacetime and that the Sudan would continue to be administered by both nations. In addition, King Fuad died in April 1936 and was succeeded by his son Faruq. At first, there were hopes that Faruq might differ from his father, for he was seen as bright, patriotic, and respectful of constitutionalism. But these expectations were ultimately not to be realized.

In 1937, the Montreux Convention ended the system of Capitulations and pledged that foreigners and minorities would now be the responsibility of the Egyptian government. The convention also abolished the Mixed Courts, though this was to be accomplished over a thirteen-year period. Finally, Britain allowed Egypt to apply for membership in the League of Nations and to set up foreign embassies and consulates around the world. For the first time since 1882, the Egyptians were permitted to create their own foreign policies and determine their own domestic affairs.

Although the treaty was accepted by a wide range of the public that thought a better military agreement impossible to negotiate, opposition to it surfaced. The military provisions were disturbing to some, who postulated that in the event of war Britain would have use of Egypt's airspace, land, and water and that the withdrawal of troops to the canal did not preclude the Royal Air Force from maintaining air bases elsewhere in the country. To others, mostly representing the left wing of the political spectrum, the treaty was inadequate because British troops were to remain in Egypt for an additional twenty years and because promises of unobstructed democracy and self-determination were absent. For the extreme right, notably the Muslim Brotherhood and Young Egypt, compromise with the occupying authorities was itself unacceptable, and the treaty was condemned.

For these groups outside the political mainstream, the treaty was viewed as an imperfect agreement that reflected the Wafd, the palace, and the minority parties' failure to answer the three basic questions of the time: the national issue, internal reform, and political representation. Moreover, the negative response that the treaty elicited signaled a growing impatience with the political center, and increasing disaffection with the Wafd, which was slowly losing its monopoly on popular politics. In the 1930s, new concepts were emerging and new organizations crystallizing that mirrored the nationalist mood in Egypt, the pains of the 1929 depression, and the growth of fascism in Europe. What is particularly noteworthy is the emergence of the Muslim Brotherhood, Young Egypt, and the rise of the antifascist groups that eventually grew into the Communist movement of the 1940s.

These emerging groups conceptualized the problems of Egyptian society and their solutions differently but were united in their rejection of Wafdist-style liberalism. Those outside the political mainstream construed the system of liberal politics as practiced in Egypt to be a form of appeasement to the British and considered this system politically bankrupt. The Muslim Brotherhood with its theocratic beliefs and Young Egypt with its blend of pharaonic[13] and chauvinistic attitudes were especially disenchanted by the vacillations of the Wafd. In opposition both to the domestic political leadership and to the British occupation, these two organizations supported Germany and Italy during World War II, thus challenging Egyptian endorsement of the Allies. This view was consistent with important sectors of the intelligentsia for whom fascism was seen as a militant form of nationalism. In addition, members of the lower and middle classes who were jettisoning liberalism and secularism as a result of the 1936 treaty and the social and economic crises damaging the country, began looking to radical nationalist ideologies imported from Italy and Germany.[14]

In striking contrast, the left-wing and antifascist movements' allegiance to the British, French, and Soviet efforts to defeat nazism was unmistakable. These movements championed the causes of democracy and world peace, and they underscored the need for reform in Egypt. Their views were expressed in both lawful cultural groups and illegal political organizations. In addition, the Wafd stood righteously in the Allied camp and came to be seen in the early 1940s as one of the most pro-British parties in the country.

By the mid-1930s, the appeal of capitalism had been tarnished internationally as a direct result of the economic and political crises occurring in the West. Simultaneously, the Wafd, which modeled itself on the parties of the Western capitalist world, was in turn weakening in Egypt. The political trends present in Europe began to be echoed in Egypt, suggestive of a general decline in local adherence to the practice of Egyptian-style liberalism. In particular, a nascent left-wing intellectual movement emerged in Egypt and was born out of the European crises of the 1930s; increasing alienation was also to frame itself in religious fundamentalism. Similarly, the discipline and self-esteem demonstrated by the fascist states inspired adherents in Egypt. In 1937–1938, the Wafd founded the Blue Shirts, a paramilitary organization, to offset the fascist Green Shirts organized earlier by Young Egypt.

At this time, the vocabulary and style of Egyptian politics was gradually changing. Even some of the actors were new, attesting to the fact that the young tradition of pluralism was operating with some effectiveness, at least below the highest levels of political life. That the Muslim Brotherhood, Young Egypt, and Socialist and Communist groups could emerge in Egypt and at times flourish was testament to the tenacity of popular activism in spite of both structural and social obstacles. The anticonstitutional behavior exhibited by high-ranking Egyptian officials should not obscure the fact that a multitude of political voices were being raised in the late 1930s, 1940s, and early 1950s and that nonestablishment, nonelectoral politics was captivating significant numbers of people below the upper echelons of political elites.

In other countries of the Arab Middle East and in Iran, for example, political diversity was either much less established than in Egypt or entirely lacking. The Egyptian Constitution of 1923 was in fact distinct because it legalized political activity. At the lower levels of the community and particularly among the urban bourgeoisie, the petty bourgeoisie, and the working class, political involvement was becoming more of a reality. Compelling people to participate was, unquestionably, the still-unresolved national issue that fanned a social and economic discontent already festering in Egyptian society—something that went virtually unrecognized by the political establishment.

With the outbreak of World War II, Britain began directing more attention to internal Egyptian affairs. Egypt was strategically vital to Britain's wartime operations, and the Egyptian government's cooperation was essential in stationing and supplying the Allied forces and in putting all the resources of the country at the disposal of the British military effort. In keeping with its treaty obligations, Egypt was placed under martial law in 1939. Censorship was instituted, and diplomatic relations with Germany and Italy broken. Egypt also accepted some half million Allied troops during the course of the conflict. Although the

Anglo-Egyptian Treaty stipulated that the number of British troops would be limited to ten thousand in peacetime, no provisions addressed a wartime situation.

Initially, the majority of Egyptians expressed no desire to become entangled in what was perceived as a war between the Western powers. Moreover, some assumed that the British would rout the Germans during the early months of the battle, but the fall of France changed people's perceptions. After that time, the Germans began to look stronger; they appeared as a counterbalance to the British, and local support for them increased. Within the population were some who knowingly advocated the fascist cause. But others looked forward to a German victory for different reasons. They were not espousing German-style anti-Semitism or, for that matter, European fascism. Instead, they were voicing a protest against the British occupation that they held responsible for the absence of autonomy and the lack of development in their own country. A pro-Axis current emerged that applauded Marshal Rommel when he landed in the western Egyptian desert and engaged the Allies at al-Alamayn. The group viewed this battle as the first step in the liberation of Egypt from British control. The British ultimately, however, defeated the German forces in this clash.

Axis propaganda was available in Egypt, having infiltrated into the country before the start of World War II through German staff officers, diplomats, and Nazi dignitaries who visited Egypt trying to attract nationalists to their cause. In addition, Italian and German spokespersons could be heard on radio sets in Egypt. When local politicians sided with the Axis powers, they had been influenced by the propaganda and roused by the charisma of both Hitler and Mussolini. A number of Egyptian political officials even began secret talks with the Nazis, and some military personnel, including Aziz Ali al-Misri and Anwar al-Sadat, made efforts to join Rommel and the Nazi war campaign.

The Allies were concerned about the implications of Axis support in Egypt, and they were specifically alarmed by Egypt's refusal to declare war on the Axis powers. Fearful that the Allied war effort was being undermined, Britain took action. Initially, Britain forced the dismissal of Chief of Staff Aziz Ali al-Misri and Prime Minister Ali Mahir owing to their fascist sympathies and the influence they commanded in society. The Egyptians were resentful, but Britain presumed it was acting legitimately because of the international threat posed by the fascists. The British expected compliant behavior from the Egyptians. Some of the British establishment envisioned the Egyptians conducting themselves as a loyal ally and accepting the terms of the Allied forces. Other British personnel perceived the Egyptians as conquered subjects. From the perspective of the Egyptians, this nuance hardly mattered. According to Muhammad Naguib, military hero and president of the Republic after 1952, British troops acted in an offensive manner that did not endear the Allies to the local population: "Their troops marched through the streets of Cairo singing obscene songs about our king, a man whom few of us admired but who, nevertheless, was as much a national symbol as our flag. Faruk was never so popular as when he was being insulted in public by British troops, for we knew, as they knew, that by insulting our unfortunate king they were insulting the Egyptian people as a whole."[15]

On a political level, Britain's intrusion into Egypt's domestic affairs climaxed on February 4, 1942, when the British forced the king to appoint the Wafdist leader, Mustafa al-Nahhas, prime minister and to approve a wholly Wafdist government. Because February 4 stands out as a landmark in Egypt's modern political history, the events that occurred on that day warrant explanation.

Husayn Sirri, an Independent, was the Egyptian prime minister until his resignation on February 2. He had supported the Allies and had cordial relations with both the palace and the British. Sirri voluntarily opted to withdraw from the political scene because he felt powerless to deal with an increasingly volatile population that suffered from food shortages, high prices, and the profiteering associated with war. He was also unable to mollify the mass of Egyptians who, in general, were culturally estranged from the libertine practices (drinking, sex) of the occupying forces, and who held the Europeans responsible for actions that were thought to corrupt elements of the local population. Anti-British demonstrations in the streets and at al-Azhar and Cairo Universities were indicative of the opposition felt throughout Egypt.

In a meeting with King Faruq on February 2, British ambassador Sir Miles Lampson criticized Egypt's flirtation with the fascists and put forward his country's ultimatum: the British demanded the formation of an Egyptian government loyal to the 1936 treaty, strongly supported by the people, and headed by al-Nahhas as leader of the majority party. Al-Nahhas was a known antifascist and for that reason was trusted by the British. Although he could never match Zaghlul's ability, or his popularity, he was the Allies' best choice. Since al-Nahhas had inherited the nationalist mantle from Zaghlul, Britain expected the population to approve his tenure.

The king and Lampson negotiated for two days, during which time Faruq lobbied for an interim coalition government under al-Nahhas, rather than an exclusively Wafdist one. During the discussions, the Allies became more and more alarmed by the critical situation in the western desert. This prompted Lampson to act. On February 4, he sent a message to Faruq saying, "Unless I hear by 6:00 P.M. today that al-Nahhas has been asked to form a government, His Majesty King Faruq must accept the consequences." When Faruq had not complied by 9:00 that evening, Lampson, accompanied by British military officers, paid a visit to the palace. A column of tanks and several hundred motorized troops surrounded the building. At the meeting, the king was offered his abdication papers or the chance to approve the appointment of al-Nahhas. The king had no choice but to give in to British pressure.

No doubt, the king viewed the ultimatum as an abrogation of

the Anglo-Egyptian Treaty, and an insult to the independence of the country. From the Allied perspective, however, the British could not in good conscience allow the Egyptian government to take on a fascist coloring: for the Allies, intervention was a necessity. Moreover, Britain expected al-Nahhas to be able to resist perpetual palace interference and govern according to the rules of the Constitution of 1923. As for al-Nahhas, he probably accepted the premiership in the hope of extracting for Egypt material assistance from Britain; he may also have wanted to undermine the minority parties' alliance with the palace.

The events of February 4, however, proved disastrous for all groups involved. When al-Nahhas accepted power through the strength of British bayonets, the party that viewed itself as the supreme nationalist body in Egypt, and that unflaggingly supported parliamentarianism, violated the Egyptian Constitution and lost its nationalist and patriotic standing in the country. Wafdists might have thought they were manipulating the British and the king, but the party's younger guard was disappointed and never forgave al-Nahhas for the supposed national humiliation to which he acquiesced. After this time, the Wafd was no longer a hegemonic nationalist power. Moreover, the British forfeited the little goodwill they had left, because their coercive action confirmed that Egypt's independence was nothing more than a sham.

Throughout the war, Egypt made an important contribution to the Allied effort, but the country remained neutral until February 26, 1945, when the government finally declared war against the Axis powers. It did so because Egypt wanted to participate in the conference in San Francisco where the Great Powers were to submit their proposals to the other countries that had declared war against the Axis and prepare for the establishment of the United Nations. Egyptians were hoping to be rewarded for their support by a British declaration of complete independence at war's end. Instead, they were again disappointed by Britain's reluctance to change the status of the country, despite efforts at negotiation, and the Labour government's plan to move ahead cautiously with moderate Egyptian nationalists. The national question, which showed no signs of resolution by the war's end, catalyzed the discontent that already existed in Egyptian society. The painfully slow movement toward social and economic reform, the sensational behavior of the king, and the publication of the so-called *Black Book* that had implicated al-Nahhas and his wife in corruption pushed the population farther away from the political center. Widespread demonstrations after the war reflected the nation's impatience with the British occupation and the lack of responsiveness exhibited by mainstream politicians. By 1946, the situation was explosive, and the three turbulent weeks between February 9 and March 4 were a product of a heightened consciousness that evolved during the years of the conflict.

Essentially, after the termination of press censorship and the abolition of martial law in August 1945, the clamor for independence began immediately. In December 1945, Prime Minister al-Nuqrashi called for fresh negotiations with the British, but an acceptable agreement was not forthcoming. In response to the seeming futility of the negotiation process, demonstrations were staged in Cairo, Alexandria, and the provinces in early February 1946. On February 9, students called a massive strike. They massed by the thousands and marched from the university grounds in Giza toward Abdin Palace, chanting, "Evacuation: No negotiation except after evacuation." When they reached the Abbas Bridge, which they needed to cross to reach the palace, they clashed with the police. The police opened the bridge while students were crossing it, causing the deaths of over twenty students by drowning and eighty-four serious casualties.[16] In protest against the police's behavior, demonstrations erupted in parts of Mansura, Zagazig, Aswan, Shabin al-Kom, Alexandria, and Cairo.

Al-Nuqrashi was forced to resign and was succeeded by Ismail Sidqi. The "street" was active in the cities and in the towns, and the growing participation of members of the working class, the petty bourgeoisie, and the bourgeoisie in the political arena was increasingly evident. The question was how to coordinate the diverse parts of the nationalist movement to express public outrage against the government and the continued occupation. The answer was found in the National Committee of Workers and Students (NCWS), which saw itself as a broad front of nationalists, democrats, progressive Wafdists, workers, and students and which carried out the general strike of February 21 and the March 4 day of mourning.

On February 21, communications workers stopped their work, gathered together in Giza, Shubra al-Khayma, and Abbasiyya, and began moving toward downtown Cairo. Workers from the railway union and the workshops of Abu Zaabal, from the pharmaceutical and woodworking industries, and from textile factories and commercial shops in Helwan, Imbaba, and Ghamra started marching toward Cairo. Students from the university, from al-Azhar, and from lower schools proceeded first to Midan al-Opera, then to Midan al-Ismailiyya.[17] Sharif Hatata, who witnessed the demonstration, later wrote in a quasi-autobiographical novel: "The streets had become rivers, rivers of people flowing from the outskirts of the city to its center. Rivers of life that had welled out from their subterranean sources in the factories, the colleges, the schools, from every place in which men and women toiled to live. . . . The rivers carried white sails inscribed with the hopes a nation. . . . Thousands of fists were raised to the sky. Voices cried out their slogans and were answered by a roar from the crowd."[18]

The demonstrators were peaceful until British armored cars, obviously unwelcome in the area, passed through the square. The crowd attacked, the British opened fire, and the protestors responded by destroying foreign shops and clubs and by attacking the British military camp. At the end of the day, twenty-three were dead and twenty-one wounded. On the March 4 day of mourning to commemorate these martyrs, newspapers were not printed, coffee shops, stores, and factories were closed down, and schools and universities remained silent. Cairo passed the day quietly, but clashes in Alexandria left twenty-eight more dead and hundreds wounded.

These events symbolized the willingness of the people to engage in political activity. Although not constituting disciplined political opposition, these protests did express the radical social and political changes that followed World War II. However, because the NCWS lacked both a stable organizational structure and political clarity, it was only of temporary importance and, once the excitement of February had faded, an easy target for liquidation by the government.

In July 1946, essentially in retaliation against the NCWS, Prime Minister Sidqi arrested hundreds of journalists, intellectuals, political and labor leaders, students, and professionals on trumped-up charges of Communist activity. In addition, he ordered the dissolution of eleven political, cultural, and labor organizations and closed down left-wing and Wafdist journals. Sidqi pretended to have uncovered a Communist plot to overthrow the existing regime and hence ordered the mass arrests. Of course, he used the word *communist* quite loosely, applying it to all of a liberal or radical bent who tended to criticize or wanted to alter the Egyptian status quo.

After his opposition was arrested, Sidqi took advantage of the calm in Egypt and flew to London to resume withdrawal negotiations with British foreign secretary Ernest Bevin. Sidqi seemed to be in a prime position to negotiate, for he was considered by the British to be an able statesman and one who could convince the king and the political parties to approve a new agreement. When Sidqi met with Bevin in October, both sides were optimistic that progress could be made. Indeed, after hard negotiations, new terms were drawn up. All parties agreed that Britain would leave Egypt within three years, that a joint Anglo-Egyptian defense pact would be established, and that the Sudan would remain under the crown of Egypt until self-government could be established. Still less than a grant of full independence, the agreement met with opposition in Egypt; likewise, it faced criticism in Britain because the pro-Sudanese lobby thought Egypt had gained too much. In consequence, Sidqi was forced to resign, and a chapter in Anglo-Egyptian history ended. The British could not again find an Egyptian leader capable of resolving the two sides' mutual differences over evacuation and the administration of the Sudan.

Al-Nuqrashi returned to the prime ministry. He took Egypt's case before the Security Council of the United Nations in 1947 to appease nationalist feelings in the country and to defend Egypt's interests. His voice was barely heard, and the council recommended a resumption of negotiations, to the extreme disappointment of all political groups in Egypt. This type of ineffectual performance made it increasingly clear that the traditional parties were incapable of solving the national question.

National pride was further bruised by Egypt's performance in the Palestine War of 1948. The population became even more alienated from Egypt's political leadership as a result of the "munitions scandal," in which defective military equipment left over from World War II had been purchased by the palace, high military officials, and some politicians and supplied to Egyptian troops fighting in Palestine. The unscrupulous behavior of supposedly respectable government officials and the embarrassing weakness of the Egyptian army precipitated the formation of the Free Officers movement by young, low-ranking military officers who felt themselves betrayed by their superior officers and political leaders.

Obviously, the Palestine War had important implications for Egypt. It meant the imposition of martial law, the resumption of antidemocratic measures, and the opening of concentration camps for left- and right-wing opposition elements. The war allowed King Faruq to restore himself, temporarily, to the role of national leader by diverting the attention of the population away from local problems and toward the foreign conflict. The war also fueled a limited racialist attack in Egypt against local Jews, which the king did nothing to inhibit.

Although the late 1940s was a dark period for constitutionalism in Egypt, the 1950s marked a dramatic improvement in the political situation, occasioned by the return of the Wafd to power in 1950. Al-Nahhas assumed the premiership and held the position for two years. During this time, the Wafd responded to the increasing pressure exerted from below and began to address some of the glaring inequities in Egyptian society. Al-Nahhas appointed the famed writer Taha Husayn as minister of education and elevated Ahmad Husayn (no relation) to the ministry of health. Both these public figures brought some improvement to Egypt's indigent population. Taha Husayn abolished tuition in state secondary and technical institutions, and Ahmad Husayn designed a social insurance system for widows, orphans, the old, and the infirm.

At this time, conditions became ripe for a renewal of decisive political activity. The nationalist and anticolonialist movements were reactivated, the university campuses were alive with political militancy, workers' strikes multiplied throughout the country, the peace movement rallied, and oppositional forces now released from prison began to rebuild their strength. Once more, the Egyptian population displayed its activism in spite of the king's continued manipulations and the Wafd's belated efforts to reform. In fact, with the Wafdists firmly in power, and controlling 228 out of 319 seats in Parliament, there was renewed hope for change. Regrettably, those expectations went largely unfulfilled because of continued corruption in the government, intraparty feuding, and the Wafd's questionable practice of appeasing the palace to avoid being dismissed from power. Because the king's behavior was so outrageous and unpalatable, he and the Wafd lost popular support.[19]

When al-Nahhas came to power, relations between the Wafd and the British were badly strained. In November 1950, al-Nahhas repeated his view that the 1936 treaty had lost its validity, that total evacuation was essential to Egyptian independence, and that the unity of Egypt and the Sudan must be respected. The British position was virtually inflexible; British officials refused to withdraw the occupation forces from the region, citing the strategic importance of the Suez Canal Zone to Britain. This rationale was not only scorned in Cairo but also incited indignation. British intransigence impelled al-Nahhas in October 1951 to declare the 1936 treaty to be null and void. With this action, the opposition was again unleashed and for the next three months dominated the political scene: the mainstream of the Wafd lost control as tension mounted in a population that called for the final removal of British troops from Egyptian soil.

The Suez Canal Zone—the last physical vestige of the occupation—became the focus of the nationalist movement. Although the zone was, of course, located within Egyptian national boundaries, it had been all but relinquished to the British occupation forces after 1936. British military installations had been built on the site, and thousands of troops were stationed on the base. With the termination of the 1936 treaty, concerted anti-British guerrilla activity commenced, taking the form of a loose-knit alliance among the Communist parties, the Muslim Brotherhood, the Socialist party (formerly Young Egypt), and the left wing of the Wafd. Presenting a "united front," antiestablishment left- and right-wing political forces engaged in the Battle of the Canal Zone, which was waged between October 1951 and January 1952. The guerrillas' main tactic was to undertake quick, sudden strikes in the dark and leave the scene before the British were able to prepare retaliatory measures.

The British were being attacked in other ways as well. Answering an appeal from the Wafdist government, eighty thousand Egyptian workers and office employees left their relatively high-paying British-affiliated jobs, paralyzing the workings of the Suez Canal base. Additionally, workers deserted British factories throughout the country. Railway workers, customs officials, airline employees, and longshoremen refused to handle

British supplies. Tradesmen refused to honor their business contracts.

As the self-confidence of the guerrilla and antiestablishment groups grew, the weakness and insecurity of the Wafd intensified, but the party was not as yet completely crippled. After the British virtually destroyed the village of Kafr Abdu in the fighting, a furious Wafdist government took speedy, symbolic, and diplomatic action, expelling the British members from the prestigious Gezira Sporting Club and threatening both to break all diplomatic and trade ties with London and to recall the Egyptian ambassador.

Although Anglo-Egyptian relations had obviously become highly confrontational by this time, the battle came to its height in January 1952. On January 19, when Egyptian commandos struck at Tel al-Kabir, the largest British garrison for materials and munitions in the Middle East, a twelve-hour battle ensued during which fifty or sixty of the Egyptian forces were killed. Violence continued on January 25 when the British attacked the police station in the city of Ismailiyya, a center of anti-British activity. Again, about fifty Egyptians lost their lives.

When news of the deaths reached Cairo, great crowds protested. Workers, students, intellectuals, and soldiers demonstrated in open challenge to the government and the British. On Saturday, January 26, a general strike closed all factories in the country. Students from the universities and al-Azhar marched on the center of Cairo and joined forces with workers gathering from the suburbs. Fires were started in symbolically significant locations: first, a Cairo cabaret was set ablaze, and then arson spread to a number of foreign businesses, department stores, cinemas, night clubs, and the Shepheard's Hotel. The crowds were incited, and Cairo burned. The torching of Cairo has been asserted, especially by Egyptian scholars,[20] to be the work of members of the Socialist party upon the recommendation of the palace.[21] The Wafd was dismissed from power, and Ali Mahir assumed the prime ministry. The Wafd left power having failed. The party had sought to preside over a truly independent Egypt, but instead, the old regime was being dismantled and coming to an end.

At this time, however, still no organization in Egypt was capable of coherently marshaling popular disaffection. A crisis in government existed: no stable party or coalition could preside from above, and at the same time, radical change was demanded from below. The weakness and disorganization of the regime was reflected in the fact that from January to July 1952, four cabinets succeeded one another.

On July 23, 1952, the Free Officers came to power in a bloodless coup d'etat, directed against various elements of a corrupt and manipulating ruling class. The coup's leaders, who were all military men, abolished the monarchy, limited the power of the landlords, sought to eliminate corruption, and at last successfully negotiated with the British under the banner of Egyptian nationalism. Later, when the military officers had penetrated into all areas of Egyptian life, they charted a new course for economic development and international alignment. Although Gamal Abdul Nasser, the revolution's leader, was applauded for ending foreign occupation, he did this by replacing the semiliberal society with a closed and politically straitjacketed country. Nasser brought dignity and self-esteem to his people and thus was able to maintain his leadership role in spite of his criticism of democracy.

With the consolidation of Nasser's rule came the end to liberal democracy in Egypt. The political diversity so characteristic of the 1920s, 1930s, and 1940s was rejected by the military officers. Moreover, the pluralism that existed, as exemplified by the independent activism of the population, has not been replicated to this day.

[4]
The Era of Liberal Politics

The Wafd

In the years between 1919 and 1952, Egypt was engulfed in a struggle to obtain independence and develop a national identity. During these thirty-odd years, the Wafd was the foremost nationalist body in Egypt. The party was identified with the nation because it harnessed the 1919 revolution in which people of all classes and backgrounds took part and, as the main outlet of popular political expression, championed the nation's demand for independence. It was bourgeois-democratic in ideology, secularist on the issue of church-state relations, and generally combative against the king and his allies. Although the party held power for only seven years (for several months in 1924, 1928, and 1930 and between 1936 and 1937, and 1942 and 1944, and 1950 and January 1952), the Wafd was electorally dominant whenever free elections were held.

Founded in November 1918, the Wafd was simply a national delegation claiming to represent Egypt on the issue of independence. In a short time, it became the center of an anti-British movement that stretched throughout Egypt and won representatives from all sectors of the population—from the poor peasant to the big landowner, and from the urban worker to the intellectual and merchant alike. The Wafd embodied the Egyptian nationalist spirit for much of the period between 1919 and 1952 and expressed the views and aspirations of people who believed explicitly in the legitimacy of self-rule.

The party operated as a coalition between members of the rural middle class and high-status urban groups such as lawyers, doctors, nonbazaar businessmen, financiers, industrialists, intellectuals and students.[1] The Wafd was able to win adherents, in part, as a result of its relationship with landowners, especially the village *umda*, or headman, who encouraged his peasants to support the party. The mobilization of the countryside was important to Wafdist electoral victories because the rural population followed the direction of its local leaders—the administrative officers, the schoolteachers, and especially the landlords. In recognition of the loyalty of the rural middle class, the Wafd ensured the continual reelection of the faithful *umda* and avoided the issue of land reform.

Although the Wafd's reliance on this rural relationship committed it to the maintenance of the rural status quo, the party was never one-dimensional. The Wafd was also supported by the *effendiyya*, who were the professionals and civil servants, and by sections of the petty bourgeoisie and groups of workers in the towns.

Ideologically, the party never sponsored radical changes in socioeconomic policy, but rather urged gradualism and moderation. Wafdist leaders kept the nationalist movement on a parliamentary path for most of the liberal era and promised to use existing constitutional and political channels to ameliorate the country's acknowledged poverty, ignorance, and backwardness. In fact, some accomplishments were achieved during the short periods of time that the party ruled: of particular significance were the improvements in the educational system, the passage of labor legislation, and the creation of the Farm and Cooperative Bank to assist small landowners. But never, whether in power or out, did the Wafd support reforming the system of land ownership or nationalizing any sectors of the economy. As well as trying to keep popular political activity episodic and circumscribed, the party also favored the ideological and socioeconomic positions that were held by the majority of the Egyptian elite.

The Wafd accepted the established and globally recognized system of international diplomacy and engaged in the negotiating process with Great Britain as a means to win national independence. In its early years, the Wafd was never allied to the British and adopted an uncompromising anticolonialist stand. With Italy and Germany threatening the Middle East in the 1930s, and the British finally ready to acknowledge that only the Wafd had the national authority to assure mass acceptance of any multilateral treaty, the British initiated a rapprochement with the party's leaders, including Makram Ubayd, Mahmud Fahmi al-Nuqrashi, and Fath Allah Barakat—Zaghlul's nephew. Negotiating with the Wafd represented a divergence from past practice when the British considered Wafdists intemperate on the issue of national independence. By 1936, however, the British had reconsidered their relationship with the Wafd, fully believing that the latter had become a moderate and conciliatory party that had calmed down since the days of Saad Zaghlul. As a result, with help from other Egyptian political parties, the British were able to conclude with Egyptian nationalists an agreement, known as the Anglo-Egyptian Treaty, giving Egypt more control over affairs of state.

The Wafd justifiably took some of the credit for the Anglo-Egyptian Treaty. For the mass of the population, however, the agreement constituted more a symbol than a substantive change. For the average Egyptian, the British still remained in Egypt and still exerted influence in the country's political and economic affairs. This influence was made particularly clear during the war, when the British were held responsible for the material shortages the population suffered and for the stationing of Allied troops on Egyptian soil. Even though the Wafd was in power between 1942 and 1944, it could do little to solve the pressing problems of underdevelopment that certainly predated the international conflict. Still, people expected a different level of representation from the Wafd; when they failed to get it, disappointment resulted, and their support for the party weakened.

After World War II, the Wafd became a tired and unimaginative party. Its leadership had become more moderate, its relationship to the British was less aggressive, and its ability to capture the masses was diminished both by its complicity with the occupying power in the February 1942 episode and by the rise of radical ideological movements. During the war, a political opposition was maturing that held political and social ideas antagonistic to those of the old order, as represented by the Wafd. The growing presence of the Muslim Brotherhood and the Communist organizations attested to this trend and pointed to the decline of the secular and gradualist approach that characterized the Wafd. In point of fact, the leadership of the nationalist movement was gradually shifting from the Wafd to these nonparliamentary parties, and through organizing efforts and journalistic activity, they began to play a role in shaping the content of social and political discourse of the postwar period.

In contrast to the ideologically defined programs of the nonestablishment parties, the Wafd never developed a comprehensive plan to remedy the deep social and economic problems that troubled the country. As this became increasingly apparent, the population began to lose faith in the party, especially as conditions for consumers deteriorated during wartime. Thus, even when the party passed reformist legislation between 1942 and 1944 or 1950 and 1952, it could no longer convince the majority of the population that it held the country's best interests in mind. Instead, in these years of growing politicization of the people, many believed that the Wafd harbored the fear that the nationalist movement would become too radical and go beyond the existing framework of acceptable political and economic discourse.[2]

The Wafd, however, was substantially different from its political rivals, which were little more than elite formations. The Wafd could both marshal popular rural support in its electoral campaigns and organize the urban masses in street demonstrations. Its following was, in comparison to other groups, diverse. Nonetheless, the party did not operate internally as a functioning democratic organization. For purposes of policy-making and strategy, the Wafd consisted of a small group of high-ranking, upper-echelon leaders who made unilateral decisions and kept tight-fisted control over the direction of the party.

Typically, the party included the leadership and a group of elected parliamentary ministers, who were disciplined followers of the prime minister and loyal both to his orientation and to the legislation he initiated in the assembly. Additionally, the party established organizations that, though not formally connected to the party, dealt with women's, students', and workers' issues. The party also set up the important area committees on the constituency level that came into being strictly in preparation for elections and that were especially significant in organizing and winning electoral campaigns.[3]

The Wafd did not manage to mirror the European parliamentary parties whose structures it imitated. Its followers were subject to no official party orthodoxy, and its organization lacked both a formal membership and a traditional system of subscriptions. Its rank-and-file members did not attend party meetings nor contribute to the framing of policy. Ideally, a party is enriched by the input of its members, and a membership is made more aware of broad internal and international affairs as a result of its organizational affiliation. Aside from the national issue, however, the Egyptian population did not develop political sophistication through the Wafd, due to the external focus of Egyptian politics on national independence and also to Wafdist conservatism. In these circumstances, the Wafd's continued success in inspiring nationalist fervor is truly remarkable since the party had to recreate its organization every time an election was allowed. Also unlike the European parties, the Wafd was structurally unable to incorporate the popular support it generated during these infrequent electoral campaigns. Moreover, being ideologically unwilling to involve the rank and file in ongoing political debate, the party did not envision its role as that of political mobilizer and educator. Its own vested interests, which centered on winning power and successfully negotiating an end to the British presence, militated against intraparty discussion that might have focused on socioeconomic questions relevant to the more disenfranchised members of society.

Because of the internal structure of the Wafd itself, the conditions of restricted independence, and the nature of limited democracy in Egypt, the party did not impart lasting democratic features to the political system. Although the Wafd did successfully, if sporadically, mobilize the Egyptian citizenry, give people occasional opportunities to participate in the political process, and help shape the values and opinions of the population, the party was not committed to deepening the process of regularized democratic activity in Egypt by encouraging independent political thought in the population. In essence, because of its increasingly centrist positions and the bourgeoisification of the membership that occurred after World War II, the Wafd became a noncontroversial establishment party that though always winning a majority of votes in the infrequent elections held in the country, was no longer the radical party of its youth.

If, as is being argued, the premier nationalist party consistently discouraged sustained and independent mass participation in political affairs, then the characterization of the Egyptian parliamentary system as elite-run takes on a certain reality—elite in the sense that political life was controlled by a small number of functionaries, men who went through a particular experience, moved through stages of political development, embraced certain ideas, and became the people who made politics. This group of political men has been very limited. The Wafd, the largest and most popular party, formulated its political ideas and strategies from above, with input only from its most prominent members, and did not look with favor upon any autonomous political activity taking place from below. In similar fashion, the Muslim Brotherhood, Young Egypt, and the Communist movement were also controlled by small vanguards, and when the Free Officers took power, they demonstrated the concept of elitism par excellence with revolution from above.

Since a political process can be informed by and reflect national characteristics, perhaps the hierarchical and autocratic system, as well as the overbearing family structure, under which Egyptians have lived for thousands of years, have conditioned people's acceptance of authority. Moreover, especially after World War II, the parliamentary political system appeared irrevocably closed to the mass of the population. In response, many Egyptians left the mainstream political arena and joined nonestablishment groups such as the Muslim Brotherhood, the Communist organizations, or Young Egypt. Still others displaced their frustrations and vented their hostilities toward immediate superiors, such as landlords, factory foremen and owners, or office managers.

By the end of the 1940s and the beginning of the 1950s, political parties in Egypt—the Wafd included—became synonymous with massive inequality, unchecked elitism, and widespread corruption. None of the mainstream groups was able to accomplish national liberation or modernization. Even though the parliamentary system contained the trappings of a free and democratic society through the guarantees of freedom of speech, press, worship, and association, too little was achieved to convince the population of constitutionalism's advantages. Therefore, when the Free Officers executed their coup d'etat, the people did not resist. They did not protest the acquisition of power by a minority; they did not object to rule by a handful of military officers. Few grieved the loss of the democratic system (and its Wafdist representatives) since arguably only the skeleton of such a structure existed, and as constituted, the system had failed to achieve national independence and social reform.

The Wafdist Vanguard

The Wafdist Vanguard, an organization composed mainly of intellectual youth inside the Wafd party, arose after the close of World War II when Egyptian students renewed their hope for national independence. Under the leadership of Dr. Muhammad

Mandur and Dr. Aziz Fahmi, the organization attempted to radicalize the center of the Wafd party. Although subject to party policy, the Wafdist Vanguard endeavored to provide the party with a revolutionary social and nationalist program.[4]

The radical ideas issuing from the "left-Wafd," as it was sometimes called, were articulated by those outside the Wafdist leadership and reflected some degree of rupture within the party ranks. Acting as a pressure group, the Wafdist Vanguard publicized the importance of understanding the national question in world terms and identified the economic bases of imperialism. Internationally, the Vanguard looked favorably on the Communist powers and supported movements of national liberation; in Egypt, it defended the rights of the workers and peasants by criticizing what it saw as the excesses of capitalist exploitation and by exposing the abuses of rural landholding.

Influenced by liberal and socialist thought, the Wafdist Vanguard revealed some communality with the Marxist forces that were simultaneously coming into their own in Egypt. Especially as a result of the antidemocratic measures adopted by successive prime ministers al-Nuqrashi, Sidqi, and Abd al-Hadi, the ties between the Wafdist Vanguard and the Marxists were strengthened. The Communist underground welcomed alliance between these two movements because antiestablishment activity, especially in the universities, was fortified by the combined forces. Moreover, at least one wing of the Communist movement—the New Dawn faction—had hopes of radicalizing the Wafd party itself, by penetrating the party from within the Wafdist Vanguard and fomenting dissident behavior from the inside.

The cooperation between radical Wafdists and Communists was important to the success of the National Committee of Workers and Students in 1946 and the National Popular Front in 1947 and generally increased the radical content of left-Wafdist publications. That traditionally sectarian Egyptian Communists felt comfortable enough to write in Wafdist papers is in fact a measure of their mutual integration.

The National Popular Front, which was an expression of left-wing disappointment with the failure of the Egyptian delegation to win recognition of the nationalist struggle before the Security Council in 1947, is a good example of the rapprochement mentioned earlier. Although not lasting long, the front did bring the opposition closer together and clarified the issues causing disenchantment. The program of the front was approved by the Wafdist Vanguard, radical workers, leftist women, and the Democratic Movement for National Liberation, an underground Marxist organization. The front demanded that Britain evacuate the Nile Valley militarily and treat Egypt as a truly independent nation by allowing it to control its own economic and political interests. The front also denounced Egyptian involvement in any military pacts involving the United States or Great Britain and recommended instituting economic measures that would improve the conditions of the populace.

At a Friday prayer service at al-Azhar on August 22, 1947, the National Popular Front demonstrated in protest of the occupation. Thousands of Egyptians, led by members of the front, thronged the Cairene mosque and shouted, "Down with imperialism," and "Evacuation with blood." Because of the scope of the disturbance, police and soldiers were called in to silence the protestors. Meanwhile, as if a chain reaction were occurring, nationalists began spilling out of mosques, cafes, and shops, gathering at Midan al-Opera to show their opposition to the British presence. When a skirmish broke out between police and demonstrators during which, as the newspaper *al-Ahram* noted, forty-five soldiers and thirty-eight protestors were killed, the police chief called for reinforcements. A summons went out from the palace directly to the Muslim Brothers, who were instructed to intimidate the radicals into submission. A state of emergency was announced in Cairo, and shortly thereafter calm returned to the city. The discontent, however, was not merely local. Demonstrations broke out in Alexandria, Suez, Shabin al-Kom, and Beni Suif. Labor disturbances also erupted among the textile workers of Shubra al-Khayma, the mechanical transport workers, and workers from the tarbush[5] industry.[6]

In the political and ideological climate of the postwar period, people from outside the mainstream of civic life were becoming increasingly active, and the experience of the National Popular Front is indicative of this trend. Again, this activity was not inspired by the Wafd; on the contrary, it was denounced by the party. This was actually the response of particular political groups that separately became convinced that the negotiation process was proving ineffective and that the establishment politicians were incapable of satisfying either the nationalist or the developmental aspirations of the population. The nonparliamentary activists, through such organizations as the National Popular Front, attempted to influence the ideological leanings of the people. However, a wide social and political gap separated the leaders of the front from the general population, and this division predetermined the downfall of the front and contributed to the ultimate inability of the radicals to effect change.

Moreover, although Communists and left-Wafdists could sporadically work together, important ideological differences divided these two groups. For most orthodox Egyptian Marxists, hostility to the West, alliance with the Socialist camp, and respect for the Soviet Union were the dominant positions. But, according to Dr. Muhammad Mandur, a prominent left-Wafdist theorist, small countries like Egypt should optimize their positions internationally by using the contradictions present between the Great Powers; dependence on one political camp was to be shunned. Moreover, whereas the Marxists at least theoretically called for the working class to lead the popular movement, the left-Wafdists envisaged intellectuals playing the avant-garde role. The Vanguard asserted that educated Egyptians would draw the people out of the quagmire in which they found themselves. In essence, the Vanguard adopted at best a diluted form of Marxist thought that made occasional shared activities possible but unity out of the question.

Advocates of left-Wafdism expressed their ideas in a number of newspapers: *al-Wafd al-Misri, Rabitat al-Shabab, al-Nas,* and *al-Bath.* In the columns of the press, and in the name of the popular classes, these advocates demanded social justice, commented on the endemic problems of poverty and ignorance, stressed the need for agrarian reform and improvements in workers' conditions, and called for the internationalization of the Egyptian national problem. In particular, *Rabitat al-Shabab* and later *al-Nas* were read as Wafdist Vanguard publications and reflected the opposition group's positions. They remained in existence until 1952 when the military coup changed the nature of political expression in the country.

The Minority Parties

Although substantive political and intraclass conflicts existed in the Egyptian political arena, personal rivalries among the politically active were also common. Moreover, the individual differences in temperament and philosophy that were present within the political vanguard were fueled by self-interested monarchs, who consistently appointed prime ministers who did not represent the electorally victorious party. Since political hopefuls were forced to contend with the reigning monarch's preferences and inclinations and could not depend on the electoral system to determine the outcome of contests or the direction of an administration, disagreements between parties often took on a personal intensity. It is not surprising then that divisiveness, which far exceeded the normal competition found in functioning parliamentary systems, became a dominant feature of Egyptian public life.

The political parties that stood as rivals of the Wafd were often called minority parties, since they customarily had little support among the people and were essentially founded as vehicles through which leading politicians could be elected to Parliament. Often little more than splinter groups of the Wafd, they were characteristically set up in response to the Wafd after important members were expelled or chose to leave because of personal or ideological conflicts.

The Liberal Constitutionalist party was founded in 1922 by erstwhile Wafdists and included as some of its most important adherents Ahmad Lutfi al-Sayyid, Adli Yakan, Ismail Sidqi, and Muhammad Husayn Haykal—distinguished intellectuals and political officials who had fundamental disagreements with Saad Zaghlul. With this list of Egyptian celebrities, the party came to be known more for its notable membership than for its popularity or its accomplishments. Although the party's membership was composed of moderate politicians, urban middle-class professionals, and landowners, its leadership consisted mainly of large landlords.[7]

The Liberal Constitutionalists were nationalists, but moderately so. The party's plan was to engage in gradual and low-keyed negotiations with the British for national independence, in marked contrast to the incorrigible attitude and uncompromising strategy characteristic of Zaghlul's Wafd. The Liberal Constitutionalists self-consciously adopted a controlled nationalist agenda to separate themselves from their rivals in the Wafd. Like the Umma party of pre–World War I Egypt, to which it was something of an heir, the Liberal Constitutionalist party presumed that Egypt, itself a legitimate national entity, had no need to make Pan-Islamic alliances. And as the name suggests, the party also believed that the long tradition of autocratic rule was outdated and had to be replaced.

The party leadership had high hopes for the Constitution of 1923, expecting the document to act as something of a restraint against the absolutism of the king. Precisely through such a political and administrative device as this, the party hoped the Egyptian nation could conduct its domestic affairs and settle any international conflicts. The Liberal Constitutionalists had every confidence that the constitution would accomplish two objectives: encourage important changes to occur internally through improvements in personal rights, health, literacy, commerce, agriculture, industry, and labor affairs; and allow for full independence and freedom without interference from any local or foreign power. As Afaf Lutfi al-Sayyid Marsot, a student of this period, wrote: "These men, as children of the Enlightenment, shared a belief that problems could be solved by rational discussion, and the British were credited with a rational approach to politics, whereas the Turkish King was believed to lack that quality and to be motivated by self-interest and personal feelings. It took them some time to realize the truth of Lord Palmerston's adage that countries are motivated by self-interest, not by reason."[8]

Essentially acting in the interests of large landowners and marked by an aristocratic image, the Liberal Constitutionalists had little connection to the masses. Although they believed that the masses would gain from their paternalistic approach, the living conditions of most of society did not significantly improve during their terms in office. Despite their regard for the Constitution of 1923, the Liberal Constitutionalists were no more tolerant when in power of opposing political trends and no wiser at governing than the Wafdists they criticized.

Another political formation, the Ittihad (Unity) party, was established in 1925 as the king's own conservative body. At that time, the king insisted that Egypt was not ready for constitutional government and that it required several more years of firm autocracy. To further his own power and to manipulate political life by ruling Egypt arbitrarily, the king established the Unity party. As a reward for those who joined the monarch's side, he elevated party leaders—there were very few members—to high political positions through royal decree. In this way, the king undermined the nascent parliamentary system and kept a decisive hand in the affairs of state. In his lack of faith in the ability of indigenous Egyptian political actors to effectively rule the country, the king resembled the British. At the beginning of the liberal age, neither force allowed parliamentary politics to take root.

Ismail Sidqi, one of Egypt's most ambitious politicians, established the conservative People's party (Hizb al-shaab) in 1930. More a clique than a political party, it was set up to support Sidqi's own political aspirations and to undermine the interests of the Unity and Wafd parties. Like many other groups in Egypt, the People's party had few members. Those who chose to associate with Sidqi, large landowners in the main, did so for self-serving purposes; essentially, they expected to benefit from the positions of patronage that he was able to distribute. The party was really an artificial formation, for although it had a program and a newspaper to publicize its views, it was little more than a few voices backing up the autocratic tendencies of Sidqi himself.

Throughout the liberal age, Sidqi was a force to be considered. He entered the political arena as a supporter of Zaghlul's but left the Wafd to help found the Liberal Constitutionalist party. In 1925, he served as minister of the interior, representing the Liberal Constitutionalists. After founding his own People's party, he became prime minister in 1930 and again in 1946. He helped negotiate the Anglo-Egyptian Treaty in 1936 and served as president of the Association of Industrialists, an organization interested in promoting capitalism in Egypt.

Political parties that expressed the opinions of particular individuals were common in Egypt. The Saadist party got its start when Ahmad Mahir and Mahmud al-Nuqrashi were driven out of the Wafd in 1937 in the most significant political battle that the Wafd had faced to date. In a short time, the Saadists gained prominence among the urban financial and industrial interests in the country, usually persons who had once belonged to the Wafd party. The Saadists were strongest among the members of the local bourgeoisie who were tied economically and ideologically to the Federation of Industries and Bank Misr. These members tended to be strong supporters of the doctrine of economic independence and naturally advocated protecting Egyptian industry. The party inherited the liberal nationalist ideas of the Wafd and advocated constitutionalism, democracy, civil liberties, and some degree of social justice. Marius Deeb, who has studied the Wafd and its rivals, concludes that the Saadist party was basically a parliamentary-cadre party: it had active members and local committees whose task was to recruit notables, but the party had little mass appeal.[9]

These political parties dominated parliamentary life during the constitutional period. Their leaders often used their parties as platforms to express their own positions and as vehicles to advance their own careers. Egypt's politicians accepted this system of government. Although they may have had disputes with the king or the British or with one another for that matter, they did not on the whole try to broaden Egypt's political base by actively encouraging popular participation in the political process. In fact, when some Egyptians chose to support the nonparliamentary groups, local politicians took note, disturbed that conventional civic life could be jeopardized.

As a group, these parliamentary political officials disappointed the population in the 1920s and 1930s when the most ardent desire of the people was for independence. As that hope went unsatisfied, the more activist nationalists rejected the political mainstream and began to demand greater changes in Egyptian society. During World War II in particular, the level of political awareness increased, and popular criticism of government officials became more strident as demands took on a social and economic orientation. The independent activity of the population rose perceptibly as the establishment parties forfeited their claim to represent the national good.

Radical Politics in Post-World War I Egypt

Along with the nationalist sentiment generated during the 1919 revolution, the ideas of socialism and trade unionism were also slowly gaining prominence among small circles of intellectuals and workers of both Egyptian and European origin.[10] Intellectuals were familiar with the ideas of Marx, Darwin, Robert

Owen, and Gandhi and the works of Tolstoy, Shaw, and Ibsen. They observed the nascent workers' movement that was aggressive in its economic demands and detached from mainstream political life. Workers' militancy was expressed in strikes among tram workers, railway workers, government printers, gas workers, street cleaners, and postal workers. In order to mobilize and direct the disaffected members of Egyptian society and take advantage of the dissident activity already organized, the radicals founded the eclectic Socialist party between late 1920 and early 1921. The party, which was legal and open to all shades of the Egyptian left, embraced the range of Socialist ideas: Fabianism, popularized by the gifted thinker Salama Musa,[11] social democracy, represented by the Second International; and Marxism, especially influenced by the Bolshevik Revolution.

Salama Musa was one of the first propagators of socialism in Egypt. He ideally looked forward to the establishment of a Socialist organization whose aim would be to study domestic and world conditions rather than to act on them. Unlike Musa, the supporters of the Second International were more global in orientation. Their ideas were first brought to Egypt by the sons of the elite who had traveled abroad for their education and were politicized by the Social Democratic parties in Europe. The predispositions of the Second International were reinforced by Muhammad Farid, one-time president of the Nationalist party, who had established relations between European Socialists and Egyptian intellectuals. Marxism, on the other hand, was promoted in Egypt by the writer Nicholas Haddad, who was influenced by the ideas of Eugene Debs and the American Socialists he befriended while living in the United States.

Two branches of the legal Socialist party were established, one in Cairo and the other in Alexandria. The Alexandrian group was composed mostly of members of Egypt's ethnic minorities— Greeks, Italians, Armenians, and Jews—and was led by Joseph Rosenthal, a Jewish jeweler and labor organizer. Because Alexandria was the focus of trade-union agitation and a center of radical intellectuals, it was a suitable place for the Socialist party to develop. In contrast, the short-lived Cairo group recruited mostly Egyptians, and Salama Musa was one of its members.

From the beginning, the Socialist party was criticized by the Wafd for adding an element of divisiveness into the political arena at a time when national cooperation was needed to face the British. Socialists were chastised for challenging the nationalist leadership of Saad Zaghlul at the most inopportune moment. Unlike much of the Egyptian population, the Socialists did not believe in Zaghlul and thought his ideas too limited. In contrast to the Wafd, nationalism was never the prime issue for the Socialists. From the start, they concentrated their efforts on labor activity in Alexandria and Mahalla al-Kubra, targeting the nascent capitalist system as their primary focus. They justified their intensive labor activity with the argument that the party could play the most influential role in the nationalist movement by basing itself in the organized proletariat. Therefore, the party considered its most important tasks to be the organization of trade unions and the leadership of the class struggle.

In 1922, the Socialist party entered its second stage of development and was transformed into the Egyptian Communist party. In its new guise, the party became more radicalized and even more divided; its militant swing produced a degree of dissension unknown in previous years. A new party program appeared that addressed the issue of nationalism and voiced the concerns of both workers and peasants. Yet, in its daily activities, the party continued to stress the need to establish a proletarian base and virtually ignored the rural and nationalist elements recognized in its platform. In reality, the party concentrated its energies on publishing the workers' newspaper, *al-Hisab*, and on influencing the labor movement, so that by 1923 the Communist party had established relations with twenty or more trade unions, many of them engaged in militant strike action.

Saad Zaghlul was well aware of the Communist party's activities among workers and its influence over some nationalist intellectuals. Although the left was not a major force in Egyptian society at this time, its presence proved menacing to the government. As a result, Zaghlul crushed the movement. He arrested and interned the party leadership in March 1924 for spreading revolutionary doctrines and advocating the change of the social system by violent means. In addition, he disbanded the Communist-oriented Confederation of Trade Unions, thus reducing the leftist influence in the workers' movement. In the confederation's place, a nationalist labor organization, the General Union of Labor, was formed under the leadership of Wafdist lawyers Muhammad Thabit and Zuhayr Sabri. With its leadership in jail and its relationship with trade unions undermined, the Communist party was badly weakened. When the party was finally outlawed in 1925, it had already been rendered impotent; as an organized political movement, communism temporarily ceased to exist in Egypt.

Although the Communist party could organize laborers in skilled industries, especially during the first years of its existence, its activities concentrated on European workers resident in Egypt, workers whose political ideas were more sophisticated and whose material conditions were superior to those of native Egyptians. As a result of these ties to foreign workers, the party was seen as alien and could never penetrate into the mainstream of Egyptian society. Moreover, its focus on the narrow class issue compromised its relationship to the nationalist movement. The Communists' distrust of Zaghlul and their misguided criticisms of nationalist sentiment in Egypt condemned the party to an isolated and marginal existence.

[5]
The Economic and Social Setting

The Struggle for Development

Egypt's population in 1947 was estimated at about nineteen million; slightly more than thirteen million lived in the countryside, and the remaining five and three-quarter million lived in urban areas. The overwhelming majority of Egyptians were *fallahin* or peasants, a group including landless peasants, peasants who owned plots of land too small to eke out their family's subsistence, and gradations of farmers who realized profits from the land. As a result of the structure of landownership and the division of land through inheritance, most peasants were condemned to poverty.

The vast majority of *fallahin* lived along the narrow ribbon of the Nile Valley where rich soil and water were available. Conditions for the majority were humble. People lived in primitive mud-brick dwellings shared with farm animals. Their diets were simple and frequently deficient in calories and essential nutrients. They constantly worked on the muddy earth and washed in and drank from the Nile waters. As a result, sickness was endemic. In particular, parasitic diseases afflicted 80 percent of the rural population; tuberculosis, malnutrition, and trachoma were also ubiquitous.

Although industrial development and urbanization did take place prior to the 1952 revolution, Egypt was basically a rural

6. Using water from the Nile

country with agriculture producing the greater part of the national income and providing employment for nearly two-thirds
of the labor force. Egyptian agriculture was heavily dependent
on cotton and used farming techniques dating back thousands of
years.

Farmers always relied on the Nile, but after cultivators shifted
to summer farming in the nineteenth century, the need for water
storage became paramount. The Aswan Dam was built in 1902 to
hold water that was to be used between February and July. This
dam was later improved, and other dams were built during the
twentieth century. Because land cultivation and production did

TABLE 1. Increasing Land Shortage as Experienced
by the Population, 1896–1949

Period	Population	Cultivated land in faddans	Average per person
1896–1900	9,860,905	6,871,696	.69
1911–1915	12,145,200	7,646,705	.62
1931–1935	15,260,200	8,539,306	.54
1945–1949	19,087,857	9,132,471	.48

Source: Mirrit Boutros Ghali, *The Policy of Tomorrow* (Washington, D.C.: Egyptian Embassy, 1953), 29.

not keep pace with the fast-growing population, improvement in the standard of living among peasants was difficult to achieve. Indeed, merely feeding the rising population became an increasingly serious concern to the government.

Although the area of cultivated land increased during the early 1900s, it was outstripped by the growth in population, resulting in the diminution of the average parcel of land. Table 1 demonstrates the land shortage experienced by the population. Extreme inequality in the distribution of landownership remained a significant feature of Egyptian agriculture. Using figures from 1950, the economist Rashed al-Barawi concludes that 71.6 percent of the landowners possessed only 13 percent of the total agricultural land, whereas only 2,115 persons, or less than 0.1 percent of the landowners, owned 1,181,623 *faddans* or nearly 20 percent of the cultivated area. (One *faddan* = 1.038 acres.) Al-Barawi's table, Table 2 on the next page, measures the unevenness of landownership.

Although there was a perceptible increase in the number of small landowners during the first half of the twentieth century, only about one-half of the landholders were able to live on the produce of their farms. The others supplemented their incomes by renting land from the larger landowners or by working as hired laborers for part of the year. Additionally, approximately one million landless laborers also hired out their labor.[1]

Concentration of landownership can be traced to historical,

TABLE 2. The Unevenness of Landownership, 1950

Total area (in *faddans*)	Total number of *faddans*	Number of owners	Average area per owner (in *faddans*)
Less than 1	780,246	1,981,339	.39
1–5	1,324,030	618,860	2.14
5–10	531,024	80,019	6.64
10–20	626,700	46,127	13.59
20–30	313,078	13,073	23.95
30–50	351,577	9,358	37.57
50–100	415,111	6,575	67.70
100–200	436,404	3,195	136.59
200–400	362,217	1,350	268.31
400–600	164,445	343	479.43
600–800	98,430	142	693.17
800–1,000	82,473	92	896.45
1,000–1,500	122,296	99	1,234.51
1,500–2,000	74,504	28	1,694.79
Over 2,000	277,258	61	4,545.21
Total	5,959,793	2,760,661	2.16

Source: Rashed al-Barawi, *Economic Development in the U.A.R.* (Cairo: Anglo-Egyptian Bookshop, 1970), 8–9.

political, and economic roots. During the rule of Muhammad Ali, land was owned by the state, and the Egyptian farmer had only the right to till the land. Exceptions did exist, however: Muhammad Ali distributed 200,000 *faddans* as private property to a number of dignitaries and government officials, as well as additional land to members of his family.

Another example of ruling-class acquisition of large tracts of state land is the case of Khedive Ismail. When Ismail came to power in 1863, his landed property amounted to about 15,000 *faddans*. Seventeen years later, it had risen to 950,000 *faddans*, or about one-fifth of the total cultivated land of Egypt. The Khedive also offered gifts of land to his family and to ministers, high officials, and favorites. After the British occupied Egypt in 1882,

7. Traditional irrigation method

the Khedival Estates were sold at favorable prices to influential notables as part of the settlement of debts incurred during Ismail's reign and as a way of winning the loyalty of the most prominent members of Egyptian society.

The size of landed estates increased further as a result of the economic depression during the interwar period when large numbers of small peasants were unable to maintain their possessions. Whereas the *fallahin* were reduced to landlessness, the large landlords cemented their monopoly on land. The state further strengthened the landowners' position by selling 182,623 *faddans* between 1934 and 1950: 1.7 percent went to small peasants, 7.6 percent to graduates of agricultural institutes, and 90.7 percent to big landlords.

8. Egyptian cotton field

Large landowners obviously benefited from the system of landownership in Egypt. Although they accounted for only a tiny percentage of the agricultural community, their disproportionate wealth brought them social standing in the countryside, political authority in Cairo, and economic power nationally. The most prominent rural families, often of Turkish origin, were associated with the palace and often aspired to offices of state. In addition, because of their prestige and connections, the great landlords kept agriculture free from the weight of taxation imposed on industry or commerce, making it the most remunerative section of the economy. In keeping with their economic interests, they also challenged the validity of an inheritance tax and refused to countenance any type of land redistribution.

The landowners were able to dictate policy because of the legislative power they wielded. Of the fifty cabinets formed in Egypt from that of Husayn Rushdi (April 5, 1914) to that of Ali Mahir (July 24, 1952), the average proportion of big landlord representation was 58.4 percent. This time period included Wafdist cabinets in which the majority of seats were also accounted for by agricultural interests. For example, in the cabinet of Mustafa al-Nahhas formed on February 4, 1942, large landowners held 63.8 percent of the positions; in his next cabinet of May 26, 1942, they held 64.2 percent.[2]

The large landlords lived off their agricultural wealth in princely fashion, often in Cairo or other urban areas. Because of population pressures and the lack of alternative employment, land values were consistently high, and profits to landlords were stable. Some landlords, through overseers, farmed the rich land on which the profitable crops such as cotton and sugar cane were grown and only rented the land on which the less remunerative crops— clover, maize, and rice—were raised. Others left their land in the care of tenant farmers, who collected cash rents or rents in kind, or used a system that combined both methods whereby the rent was fixed but a share of the crop was also passed to the landlord. Most frequently, the landlord provided for the cost of cultivation and received in return the majority of the produce. He regulated matters of water, drainage, and rotation and oversaw the harvesting of the crops.

Most landlords were cautious and apprehensive and invested in agriculture because its methods were safe and its results tested. As late as 1945, two-thirds of all capital invested in the economy went to agriculture and particularly agricultural land. Only a small percentage of forward-looking landowners branched out and invested in industry after the creation of Bank Misr in 1920. Bank Misr was established in particular to provide capital for

9. Lunch along the Nile

commercial and industrial development, and it financed cotton spinning and weaving, publishing, local air transport, film production, and the manufacture of pharmaceuticals. Although native Egyptians were involved in setting up the institution, many members of Egypt's ethnic minorities, some acting as agents for the large international financial firms and manufacturers of Europe, were involved in Bank Misr. And even though members of the native business community might have expressed the desire for economic independence, Bank Misr did not provide a basis for such activity. The bank was tied to multinational banks in both Germany and France and was even managed for a time by foreigners.

In fact, the nonagricultural sectors of the Egyptian economy were dominated until 1952 in large measure by members of Egypt's European minorities. Egypt depended on minority participation in its economy, especially after the country became part of the global economy in the second half of the nineteenth century. At that time, agricultural production became almost entirely geared to the cultivation and export of long-staple cotton, and Egypt embraced a money economy with even the smallest peasant affected by the world market system. As a one-crop exporter, Egypt was extremely dependent on the monopolies that controlled the financing, trading, transporting, and industrial processing of the cotton crop, and Egyptian minorities were particularly active in these areas.

From the period of Muhammad Ali until World War I, exclusive of agriculture, most of the capital invested in financial, industrial, and commercial ventures belonged either to Europeans or to those Egyptians who came from the country's religious or ethnic minorities.[3] But Egypt was largely a homogeneous country, with the majority of people being Arabic-speaking Muslims and less than 10 percent of the population composed of minorities. By far the largest minority group was made up of indigenous Coptic Christians, who accounted for between 7 percent and 8 percent of the population. The remaining non-Coptic

Christians and Jews, many possessing foreign citizenship and protection and holding Greek, Italian, French, or British passports, numbered about one-quarter of a million people.[4] This latter group played a disproportionately large role in the economy until the 1952 coup d'etat.

Although the economic activity dominated both by Europeans and by Egypt's ethnic minorities decreased during the first half of the twentieth century, these groups were still economically important. In 1919, for example, this combined group of foreigners and Europeanized Egyptians owned 91 percent of all capital invested in Egypt. The percentage of foreign businessmen investing in companies was constantly decreasing as Egyptians began to participate in the industrial process (see Table 3). Still, as Table 4 on page 84 shows, the influence of Europeans and Egyptian minorities, who for purposes of classification were considered foreign, cannot be discounted, as shown by their share in the companies (estimated in E£).

Prior to World War I, Egypt had few industrial enterprises. The country only began its industrial growth during the conflict, when a crippling shortage of imported manufactured goods compelled the establishment of local factories. Factories employing more than fifty workers were set up, especially in spinning and weaving, oil pressing, tanning, grain milling, and metalworking, to supply the domestic market as well as to equip and feed the British military population stationed in Egypt. Emerging industrialists and merchants made great profits by selling goods to the foreign soldiers. These huge fortunes made by a few profiteers contrasted to the shortages and sufferings endured by the mass of the population. The shortages of goods, the high price of all commodities, and the profit orientation of landowners who cultivated the lucrative cotton crop in place of edible wheat, together with the disruptive presence of foreign troops on Egyptian soil, wore down the Egyptian population.

Indigenous industry for a time did meet a large part of the domestic need and provided employment of both a skilled and

TABLE 3. Percentage of Foreign and Egyptian
Businessmen Investing in Companies, 1934–1948

| Year company | Percentage of investment | |
was founded	By Egyptians	By foreigners
1934–1939	47%	53%
1940–1945	66%	34%
1946–1948	84%	16%
1934–1948	78.7%	21.3%

Source: Rashed al-Barawi, *Economic Development in the U.A.R.* (Cairo: Anglo-Egyptian Bookshop, 1970), 40.

nonskilled variety. But the process of industrialization in Egypt was not without problems. Industry was faced with the narrowness of the home market due to the meager purchasing power of the mass of the population, the limited availability of local raw materials, the absence of local fuels and cheap electrical power, the short supply of technicians and skilled workers, the reluctance of Egyptian capitalists to invest in industry, and the typically unsympathetic attitude of the government. Moreover, after the end of the war, industrial activity decreased as trade with the outside world resumed.

Not until 1930, when tariff legislation was passed by the government and Egyptian industry was protected from foreign competition, did Egyptian participation in industry and trade become significant. At that time, some landowners invested in industrial enterprises, particularly those that tended toward monopoly. They became active in the sugar and cement industries, in distilleries, in chemical fertilizer industries, and especially in the Bank Misr companies. The bank was involved in everything from aviation to printing, from the film industry to the mines and quarries, from textiles to ocean shipping.

If tariff regulations initially heightened economic opportunities in Egypt, then the world depression with its accompanying fall in cotton prices devastated the economy and demanded new

TABLE 4. Estimated Share of Egyptians and Foreigners in the
Capital of Companies before the 1952 Revolution

	Egyptians	Foreigners	Total
Capital of companies founded before 1953	6,006,635	60,733,751	66,740,386
Newly established companies, 1933–1948	21,041,566	5,677,048	26,718,614
Increase in capital, 1933–1948	19,260,632	5,213,378	24,474,010
Total capital in 1948	46,308,823	71,624,177	117,933,000
Percent of capital in 1948	39%	61%	100%

Source: Rashed al-Barawi, *Economic Development in the U.A.R.* (Cairo: Anglo-Egyptian Bookshop, 1970), 40.

avenues of development. Although there was national consensus that Egypt needed to expand its limited industrial base, the industrial growth that occurred during World War II could not be sustained after the conflict's end. The strategy of import substitution that had been adopted after World War I was not improved on or replaced. Egypt in the 1940s had reached a threshold, and without intermediate and capital goods and greatly improved technology, the advancement of industrialization was limited. Although in theory industrialization was credited with the ability to solve Egypt's chronic problems, not the least of which was a growing population that was outstripping the capacity of the country's agriculture, in reality enduring structural expansion was much more difficult to achieve. Given the limitations of the land, investment, infrastructure, and technology, Egypt was mired in economic distress.

Despite expectations, the economy was little changed after the

10. Cairo lemonade vendor

war. Although Egypt was cut off for six years from its cotton markets and from the usual sources of its imported consumer goods, and although demand was considerably increased as a result of the needs of thousands of soldiers stationed in Egypt, steady industrial development could not be maintained after the resumption of normal economic and trade conditions at the end of the war. Even the activities of the Middle East Supply Center, a wartime agency founded by the British government and jointly administered with the United States to oversee the flow of civilian imports to the Middle East, only temporarily boosted industrial growth. Under the center's auspices, new industries were created and old ones expanded. The industries established included the dehydration and canning of vegetables, the production of rubber goods, the processing of jute, and the making of spare parts and tools, as well as chemicals and pharmaceuticals. The businesses that the center helped renovate and develop included textiles, preserved foods, glass, leather, cement and other building materials, petroleum, and mechanical industries. Vital in the short run, these efforts did not materialize into a major renovation of the Egyptian economy.

The wartime production resulted in an increase in the size of the proletariat and an intensification of urbanization, with peasants moving to the towns, largely from Upper Egypt to the Delta, in search of work and attractive wages. The number of factory workers rose from 247,000 in 1937 to 756,000 in 1947. The numbers of workers involved in construction, transportation, and commerce also increased commensurately. The growth of industry led to the concentration of workers in factories; in 1946–1947, 57 percent of those working in productive industries were concentrated in 583 such enterprises,[5] creating an unequaled opportunity for the growth of trade unionism.

Egyptian workers flocked to the war factories set up by the British because of the lure of unmatchably high wages, but Egyptian salaries generally declined during the war, with prices exceeding and depressing money wages. For most of the working class, however, poor wages were the result of low productivity that had its roots in malnutrition, lack of training, poor equipment, and mediocre management. The migration of peasants to urban areas also tended to lower wages for all. Even those workers fortunate enough to be employed in war-related industry were disappointed after the close of hostilities when they were dismissed by their employers. These workers joined an increasingly large and dissatisfied jobless work force that emergent radicals and trade unionists tried to engage. The politicization of the working class did progress but proved to be a difficult and complicated process.

Many factories failed after the war's end due to a resumption of foreign competition. The war did not produce a qualitative change in the level of industrialization. That is, no discernible transformation occurred from the manufacture of consumer nondurables to the manufacture of more-advanced goods. Although the Korean War provided a temporary stimulus to industry by raising the price of cotton and by increasing local purchasing power, this war was not strong enough or structurally important enough to reverse the downward trend. Egypt then had to face a failing economy. Not until after the Free Officers took power did a changed economic program bring a more active role for the government, policies of land reform, measures to relieve land scarcity, industrialization with public investment in heavy industries, economic planning, and educational and social welfare. The new rulers instituted policies that clearly separated them from the ancien régime. They destroyed the remnants of feudalism, they removed European and minority interests from large sectors of the economy, they created a public sector, and they adopted a system of economic planning.

The Emergence of New Social Forces in Egypt

World War II was a watershed event for Egypt. The war demonstrated the need for industrial advancement and temporarily hastened the proletarianization of the masses. It continued Egypt's involvement in international politics and indicated the continued dominance of the British in the Nile Valley. The war aggravated social problems and made the reality of inequality more disruptive. A social and political radicalism emerged as a result of the international conflict, affecting members of both the middle and popular classes and altering the scope of political and economic discourse. Charles Issawi, the noted economist, observes:

Egypt had done its best to stay out of the war, but it had been engulfed by the flood of propaganda pouring in from every quarter. Britain and the United States harped incessantly on the themes of democracy, social justice and perhaps the one which found the most appreciative audience, the upholding of national independence against Nazi . . . aggression. . . . The prowess of the Soviet Union was exalted and Russian economic and social achievements were given their due, and more. In these circumstances it was natural that there should be a rapid spreading of Socialist and Communist ideas, and an even greater spreading of a deep and inarticulate dissatisfaction with the existing order.[6]

Swelling the ranks of the dissatisfied were sections of the petty bourgeoisie, radical students, workers, and some women who were becoming more involved in Egypt's changing political culture. Organizationally, the beneficiaries of this discontent were the Communists, the Muslim Brothers, and the Young Egyptians. Although the newly dissatisfied sections of the populace were separately participating in anti-British activity and giving new energy to the nationalist movement, their complaints became even clearer by the war's end. They protested staggering inflation, anguishing shortages, and increasing joblessness. They witnessed the king's indiscretions, saw the Wafd weakened by right-wing factionalism, and were frustrated by the continued failure of negotiations with the British. Workers became involved in labor disputes and strikes. Students found their outlet in demonstrations and open criticism of the government. In this environment, trade unionism was strengthened, the Muslim Brotherhood gained adherents, and the illegal Communist movement grew more self-confident. Though the opposition was small in numbers, it was able to help undermine Egypt's ineffectual political system and break down its social hierarchy through demonstrations, organizational efforts, and the publication of newspapers and leaflets.

The Petty Bourgeoisie

Economic development, expansion in governmental bureaucracy, and the spread of education led to a substantial increase in the number of the petty bourgeoisie by the 1930s. This burgeoning class was composed of low- and middle-echelon government employees, small landowners, teachers, police and army officers, low- and middle-echelon employees in companies, professionals, students, small and middle traders, and artisans. Although growing numerically, the urban petty bourgeoisie found its material conditions deteriorating, the combined result of demographic pressure, price increases, and salaries not keeping pace with inflation. With a higher number of students being educated, trained, and graduated from higher institutes, job competition was stiff, and financial rewards were less available, resulting in a large group of "intellectual unemployed" young adults whose social roots were generally petty bourgeois.

Economic frustration often nourished political discontent. As a class, the petty bourgeoisie was highly nationalist. Its members resented the British occupation because this intrusion offended civic pride and denied personal as well as national growth. For some, the Wafd provided a framework within which to express nationalist sentiment. But to the more politically dissatisfied among them, the Wafd was losing its attractiveness: it came to represent only the occasional holding of elections, endless negotiations with the colonial power, and ineffectual moderation. From this viewpoint, the Wafd merely replicated the worst abuses of Western-style constitutionalism and so provided neither an entrance into politics, nor a voice in policy-making, nor an answer to the national question. The Wafd's anti-British nationalism was ultimately considered insufficient to deal with Egypt's political, social, and economic problems.

11. Muski Street, Cairo

Sections of the petty bourgeoisie became isolated from mainstream political thinking and developed into a revolutionary-
minded social force, critical of the practice of personality politics,
impatient with ruling-class resistance to social change, and jaded
by the incorrigible attitude of the British with respect to Egyptian independence. The hegemonic political parties were cen-
sured for failing to resolve the burning issues of the day: the
national question, modernization, and more-direct participation
in the political process.

A part of this class lost faith in liberalism and in indigenous
capitalism because both failed to produce significant results. For
the wings of the petty bourgeoisie that saw no future in the

established system, alternative ideas were embraced. In 1928, during the international economic crisis, the Muslim Brotherhood was established. In 1933, as European fascist forces grew bolder, Young Egypt was born. The ideas of the radical left also emerged in the 1930s and 1940s. Members of the petty bourgeoisie often populated these groups and held important positions within them. Egypt's political culture would be increasingly shaped by these forces.

Clearly, the petty bourgeoisie was not united in political orientation: all shades of thought prevailed from the extreme left to the extreme right. However, members of this social class shared in the demand for national rejuvenation, and since they could neither penetrate nor influence the existing political structure, they looked for redress outside mainstream politics.

Students

Like Egyptian society, the educational system was inherently unequal, with several systems of instruction operating during the first half of the twentieth century. Some primary schools catered to urban Egyptians intending to pursue their education in secondary school and often in university. These schools cost money and provided instruction that was vastly superior to the elementary schools that serviced the rural population and were often custodial at best. This bifurcation in the educational system contributed to the disparities between classes and geographic regions and perpetuated social and economic inequities. Social class also determined entrance into the university. According to most accounts, the majority of students in the secular universities before the 1952 revolution came from lower middle-class families in the urban areas, especially the *effendiyya*, and from middle landowning families in the rural areas.[7] University attendance was costly and often placed a heavy financial burden on families with modest resources. The fees in fact generally prevented poorer families from enrolling their offspring at all.

In addition to the educational system's "Egyptian track" that serviced the majority of the indigenous population, a "European track" for the elite or talented also existed. European education received an impetus in nineteenth-century Egypt as a result of the missionary work carried out first by French and Italian Catholics and later by British, German, and American secular and religious educators. Instruction was conducted in a foreign language, and students thus developed a skill that gave them an advantage in employment and some degree of social standing in the country. Teaching was generally of a higher level than that in local schools, and the curriculum encouraged the adoption of Western ideas. Egyptian minority groups also established private educational institutions within this latter track in Egypt, but these schools tended to attract coreligionists rather than a diversity of students. Although foreign schools fell under the jurisdiction of the Egyptian educational authorities, they were separate from their Arabic counterparts in methodology and finances.

That Europeanized Egyptians had a considerable edge in education is undeniable; their literacy rate was fourteen times greater than that of the overall Egyptian population in the first decades of the twentieth century.[8] But foreign-language institutions provided students with more than a mere facility with Western languages. They also conveyed, through both classroom experience and social interaction, modern notions of class, nation, art, and politics distilled from European and American history and thus contributed to the development of an international worldview and also to the encouragement of social criticism and political awareness.

An Islamic education was available through al-Azhar and its related institutions, schools whose curriculum was entirely independent of the secular system until the mid-1930s. Only then did the lower educational establishments, the *kuttabs*, become modeled on secular schools, a change that of course provoked controversy in Egypt. Although modernists, like the novelist and essayist Taha Husayn, maintained that al-Azhar should be accountable to the state for its educational methods and philosophy, traditionalists, like the founder of the Muslim Brotherhood, Hasan al-Banna, believed that al-Azhar, by providing a religious education unique in the world, was its own justification and should have been maintained without alteration.

Al-Azhar was important for a number of reasons, not the least being that it provided instruction for aspiring students unable to pay the cost of a secular education. Admission brought free tuition, board, and very humble lodgings during the course of study. Economic hardship was endemic among Azharites, but gaining the chance for a better future—teaching Arabic in state schools—outweighed the difficulties that had to be endured.

Since the 1919 revolution, Egyptian students had been among the most politicized groups in society. Assembled in an intellectual environment, students had the leisure to think about the issues of the day and were always concerned about the future. Student life made them extremely sensitive to political and social events, permitted the study of other countries, and encouraged freedom of thought and imagination—all of which allowed students to entertain new ideas and challenge existing ones. Students formed an avant-garde whose intellectual and ideological curiosity was always widening.

The student movement, which was nationalist, anti-British, and highly vocal, occupied a significant place in Egypt's political life. In the mid-1930s, for instance, the liberal regime was confronted by restless, dissatisfied students whose hopes for political independence and economic advance were fading. The Constitution had been abrogated by Ismail Sidqi and replaced by a less "populist" version, with democratic liberties suspended. When Tawfiq Nasim Pasha took over the government in 1934, students anticipated a return to the ideals of 1923. But backed by the British, Tawfiq only restored the Constitution in modified form, a gesture that enraged the student population.

In November 1935, the students took their rage to the streets of Cairo and other large cities. A clash between protestors and the police on November 14 in the capital, for example, left one student immediately dead and another so badly injured that he died in the hospital days later. Demonstrations continued in December and gained the support of trade-union members and professionals alike. Student protests provided a framework for otherwise powerless youth to press for national independence and call for the restoration of the Constitution. Growing student activism may have sent a message to the government and possibly even contributed to the formation of the United Front, which brought all of the political parties together and ultimately negotiated the Anglo-Egyptian Treaty of 1936. Youth and student groups proved that they could act as a positive and decisive force in Egyptian politics.

Although the student movement until World War II remained basically Wafdist in orientation, Wafdist hegemony began to wane as a result of the 1935-1936 student protests; the young were captivated by more-dissident political tendencies. Young Egypt was the first oppositional group to compete with the Wafd for student support. Shortly after being formed in 1933, Young Egypt began to attract students into its ranks. By 1934, some 40 percent of its membership was accounted for by students. Students belonging to Young Egypt participated in the protests of 1935-1936, and they successfully fielded candidates for student representatives in the Faculty of Law and the Faculty of Arts elections of 1937. Between 1941, when the organization was suppressed, and the late 1940s and early 1950s, when it was transformed into the Socialist party, Young Egypt's strength in the university had weakened. But it remained a force, especially when linked to its closest ideological ally, the Muslim Brotherhood.

From the beginning of its organization, the Muslim Brotherhood took the recruitment of students seriously and considered them the organization's "striking force." According to Ahmed Abdalla, who has written convincingly about the student movement, Hasan al-Banna maintained a close relationship with many of the students and inspired in them something approaching reverence. Abdalla notes: "He [al-Banna] maintained personal contact with them and knew in detail about their interests and activities and even their personal lives. He was particularly concerned about their academic progress and encouraged them to devote themselves to their studies at the time of their examinations. Student members of the Brotherhood were organized in 'families' which met regularly every week in the house of one of them to study an Islamic educative syllabus specially designed to suit their age group and educational level."[9]

In the Brotherhood's early years, most of its student members came from al-Azhar. However, after al-Nahhas became prime minister in February 1942 through British insistence, the Brotherhood began to agitate more actively in the secular institutions among students disenchanted by Wafdist conciliation. After World War II, the Brotherhood played a consistently active role in university politics. Its candidates stood for election to the student unions of the different faculties and were often victorious. Membership in the highly organized, paramilitary Rover Scouts aided the Muslim Brotherhood's campaigns by intimidating and threatening political opponents.

The Communist groups that emerged during World War II were also active among students. Because no united Communist party existed in Egypt during this period, internecine competition between rival Communist organizations often hindered their effectiveness. Despite fractiousness among the Marxists, a so-called progressive alliance of Wafdists and leftists did come into being after the war to counter the activities of the Muslim Brotherhood and Young Egypt, which were the alliance's main competitors in the university.

An important Communist organization at this time, Iskra, recruited in the institutions of learning in Cairo and Alexandria. One such place was the *lycée français*, which attracted a faculty that included Marxists, liberals, and antifascists. Often these teachers were passionately committed to democracy and the defeat of nazism in Europe, and they exposed their students to radical ideas. Students were also encouraged to attend lectures at the House of Scientific Research, the legal front for Iskra. The House of Scientific Research sought to disseminate cultural information to its members and to popularize progressive views of social justice. In reality, and on a deeper level, it acquainted people with Communist ideas under the guise of scientific and cultural research. The group numbered about three hundred members, most of whom were students and graduates. The house published a monthly periodical that contained research articles and reproductions of the lectures delivered at formal meetings. Copies of the left-wing magazines *Umdurman*, the *Vanguard*, and the *New Dawn* were also on sale.

Iskra organized aggressively in the university and stressed the issue of national liberation against imperialism. Iskra provided hundreds of students, most often from the upper echelons of Egyptian society, a way of expressing their frustrations with the traditional political parties. In the postwar period, when the nationalist movement was animated and when demonstrations, marches, strikes, and protests were frequent, students were caught up in the spirit of the times. For many radical student nationalists, a choice had to be made between the Muslim Brotherhood and the Communist organizations. Those who opted for the left-wing alternative did so because the traditional, fanatical, and restrictive orientation of the Brotherhood was unattractive. Its emotional patriotism did not provide adequate explanations for the complex of problems the Egyptians faced. Iskra attempted to offer solutions and filled a vacuum in the political arena, especially since its members were overwhelmingly drawn from Egypt's Jewish minority.[10] The largest Communist group in the university during this period, Iskra was active in the faculties of the liberal arts and scientific professions.

Another Communist group was the Egyptian Movement for National Liberation (EMNL) led by Henri Curiel. In contrast to Iskra, the EMNL recruited among the more humble members of society. It too attracted students, but many of its student recruits came, surprisingly perhaps, from al-Azhar. The Azharites knew the party had a Marxist orientation, but they did not perceive the group as atheistic because Curiel was never doctrinaire about the religious question and was content to detach religion from Marxism. The EMNL tried to understand men of religion and to use Islam as an aid in achieving a measure of progress and equality. Abd al-Rahman al-Thaqafi, for instance, a Communist Azharite, pursued the idea of studying Islam as a militant religious philosophy directed against both imperialism and internal exploitation, views that he explored in his two books, *Islam and Communism* and *The First Revolutionary in Islam*. When the Democratic Movement for National Liberation (DMNL) was formed in 1947, symbolizing a partial unification of the Communist movement, the students represented an active force in the party. They wrote for party newspapers, agitated on the campuses on behalf of their organization, and continued to recruit more members.

The leftist orientation of at least a part of the student movement was demonstrated in the postwar years in the pages of *al-Talia* (the Vanguard) newspaper. Articles about capitalism, socialism, and imperialism appeared frequently, and reports about strikes and demonstrations were regular features. After the war in the summer of 1945, students began holding meetings at the university in preparation for the beginning of the new academic year. Their intent was to politicize their contemporaries and stage continuous protests against the British occupation. In October, the students established the Preparatory Committee to the National Committee of Students for the purpose of expressing their nationalist goals and aspirations. The influence of the Marxist groups on the main points of the program was clear: the committee called for the termination of economic, political, and cultural imperialism; the elimination of the agents of imperialism, both the feudalists and the large capitalists; and the establishment of a united nationalist front to face the imperialists.

From October 1945 to February 1946, the movement elected a High Executive Committee with representatives from the different universities, institutes, and schools. The delegates came from the Wafdist Vanguard and the Communist organizations. (Members of the Muslim Brotherhood refused to join, ostensibly because of the presence of Communists, and have since been accused of undermining the nationalist movement at the request of Prime Minister Sidqi.) The High Executive Committee established links with workers, and through their combined efforts, the National Committee of Workers and Students was formed. The demonstrations of February and March 1946 were products of their joint activity. The National Committeee of Workers and Students was significant, first, because it directed the nationalist movement at the time and, second, because it represented the left's first attempt to build a political front capable of leading the masses in a revolutionary manner.[11]

The student movement in 1945 and 1946 mirrored the mood of the nation: it was restless, detached from the political mainstream, and searching for a new direction. The movement resented the king, smarted at the unfulfilled promises made by the British during the war, and was offended by the presence of the occupation forces. Throughout the late 1940s and early 1950s, student demonstrations occurred with remarkable regularity, attracting sympathizers from most regions of Egypt, from most social classes, and from varied ethnic and religious backgrounds. Although the concerned youth were rallying around the national issue, explicitly economic and social criticisms of government policy were also being made. Since neither the Wafd nor the minority parties were capable of winning independence or improving the condition of the majority of the population, the students turned to alternative political organizations. Both the Communist movement and the Muslim Brotherhood were enriched by their affiliation.

Workers

The Egyptian trade-union movement got its start in the late nineteenth and early twentieth centuries when ethnic workers of

12. Pottery sellers

Greek, Italian, and Armenian origin resident in Egypt first organized in labor unions. In the immediate post–World War I period, Egypt witnessed not only the nationalist upheaval of 1919 but also workers' militancy. Between March and May 1919, tram workers, railway workers, government printers, gas workers, street cleaners, workshop employees, and postal workers temporarily paralyzed the country's economy with continual strikes protesting their abhorrent working conditions and low wages.[12]

By 1922, 102 unions had been formed: 38 in Cairo, 40 in Alexandria, 18 in the canal zone, and 6 in the provinces. Members of many of these new associations participated in the eighty-one strikes that occurred between 1919 and 1921 protesting poor wages that had failed to keep pace with wartime inflation.[13]

The growth of trade-union consciousness was reflected in efforts to merge the various trade groups into one association. The first such attempt resulted in the formation in February 1921, of the General Federation of Labor, an organization that had close ties to the Egyptian Socialist party (and later the Egyptian Communist party) and boasted some 3,000 members. The leftist labor leaders involved in the federation disseminated anticapitalist propaganda to workers, provoked labor unrest, and even led simultaneous strikes in different industries—all as means of trying to build class consciousness. By stressing the common interests of workers in various establishments, the federation's leaders endeavored to unite scattered groups of workers.

The Wafd, in power at the time, undermined the Communist influence in the labor movement by arresting the leaders who were labelled provocateurs, by trying to marginalize the Communist party, and by setting up the pro-Wafdist General Union of Labor Syndicates whose purpose was to contain labor militancy. As a way of curbing momentum among radicals in the labor force, and in an effort to forward its own political struggle, the Wafd organized labor unions as auxiliary associations to the party and groomed moderate Wafdist labor leaders to restrain workers.

Especially in its early years, the trade-union movement suffered from the country's high rate of casual labor and a lack of solidarity between skilled and unskilled workers. The agrarian origins of the nascent industrial population, the illiteracy of the vast majority of workers, and the resistance shown by industrialists and government authorities acted as brakes on labor organization. The movement was also undermined by the differences in race and language among the workers and by their unequal standards of living; European workers (Greeks, Italians, Armenians) were paid consistently higher wages than Egyptians. Moreover, the activists in the labor movement were continually confronted by the British occupation so that political campaigns fought in the 1910s and 1920s were often directed against foreign control of Egypt and not capitalist exploitation.

Labor unions continued to grow through the 1920s, and as a result of the Great Depression of 1929, their development was pushed forward. With the economic crisis causing unemployment and a reduction in wages, workers began to understand the merits of labor organization. Consequently, by the 1930s, the mainstream political parties began to recognize glimpses of militancy on the part of workers and were interested in maintaining cordial relations. To such an end, the Wafd initially supported the aristocratic Abbas Halim's intention to found the Federation of Trade Unions in 1934.

Halim was not the most likely trade unionist. He was a direct descendant of Muhammad Ali, had been raised in Germany, joined the Imperial Guard, served in the Third Uhlan Company at Potsdam, and had been made aide-de-camp to Wilhem II. He supported Germany and then Turkey in World War I and in 1924 returned to Cairo where he became a member of Egypt's fashionable society.[14] Abbas Halim quickly alienated himself from Wafdist favor, and by 1935, ties between the two were terminated. Halim believed that labor groups should be autonomous of traditional party politics, a view that completely contradicted Wafdist tactics. After severing relations with Halim, the Wafd established the rival Higher Council of Trade Unions—the embryo of a Trade Unions' Congress—and managed to control most of the labor movement until after World War II, despite the challenges leveled against the council by Halim and the king.

For the Wafd as well as for the whole of the ruling class, independent labor groups were anathema. Labor was to be controlled by political parties in order to channel workers and temper their demands. The idea that workers could legitimately join together to defend their self-interest and attempt to improve their situations was absent. Indeed, up until World War II, the working class was considered by mainstream political parties as a subsidiary resource that could be exploited or discarded at will. The war changed political and economic life, and at that time trade unions began to emerge as an independent and highly active force.

Labor militancy was in fact one factor that convinced the Wafd in 1942 to approve badly needed changes in the laws related to workers' interests. But other issues concerned the party as well. The Wafd recognized the strategic importance of workers who could be relied on to participate in demonstrations. Additionally, because the party felt weakened by the events of 1936 and 1942 and vulnerable to attack from the right-wing parties, it needed workers' support to neutralize the criticism of its rivals. On a different but equally significant level, the Wafd's ability to control the labor movement meant that the party could prevent any attempt to halt wartime production. Thus, in an effort to pass prolabor legislation, the party recognized trade unions. Although this recognition was a major policy advance, the new labor regulation in practice only moderately improved conditions for the labor community, since restrictions on trade-union activity continued. In particular, the new law forbade strikes and organization among civil servants, government workers, domestic workers, hospital workers, and agricultural laborers, though these bans were defied on many occasions during the 1940s when workers increasingly resorted to illegal strikes.

During the 1940s, union organization was on the rise. In 1942,

200 unions were formed representing 80,000 workers in industry, transport, and commerce. In 1946, 488 unions had over 95,500 members; in 1950, union membership rose to over 148,400.[15] Along with an increase in the number of workers was a parallel rise in militancy. Workers' demands were clearly articulated and covered issues of economic and political importance.

The working class emerged as an autonomous force in the nationalist movement. During the mid-1940s, labor became active in the movement to oust the British from Egypt, and its activity was independent from traditional party politics in the country.[16] Labor's new leadership, which included Socialists, Communists, Muslim Brothers, and Independents, played an important part in raising class consciousness among rank-and-file workers. That labor militancy spread was confirmed by the large number of strikes and labor disputes that occurred among sugar workers, textile workers, railway workers, government employees, military men, and police officers between 1944 and 1952.

After the war, some workers joined the Communist underground or worked alongside it in legal front groups organized to improve working conditions and to struggle for national independence. Some trade unionists looked forward to the establishment of a labor party. But in its absence, the Workers' Committee for National Liberation, which saw itself as the political arm of the trade-union movement, championed national independence and called for the unification of the labor community. Tied to the New Dawn Communist organization, the committee published its demands in the radical workers' newspaper *al-Damir*.

At the same time, a small number of rival leftist trade unionists from competing Communist organizations tried to attract workers into their particular revolutionary underground parties. Recruitment among workers was generally limited, and the division of the Marxist movement in Egypt into a number of rival groups created factionalism in the labor movement as well. Sectarianism was evident at the World Federation of Trade Unions Conference held in Paris in October 1945 when two separate

Egyptian Communist delegations, one from the New Dawn and one from the Egyptian Movement for National Liberation, were sent to represent Egypt. At the Paris meeting, a number of resolutions were adopted, most notably the demand that workers be allowed to organize freely in unions and be granted freedom of thought, speech, press, and association. The conference called for world peace and the full independence of all countries from imperialist control. The Egyptian delegates were inspired by their experience, and they brought their enthusiasm and expectations back to their coworkers in Egypt.

Another pocket of left-wing and labor militancy was the National Committee of Workers and Students that, as mentioned earlier, led the anti-British demonstrations in February 1946. The alliance of radical workers and students momentarily excited the nationalist movement, temporarily rocked the establishment, and brought a large-scale offensive against the government. Nationalist activity significantly affected the working class, encouraging a heightened consciousness that, though political in origin, matured through the 1940s into a socioeconomic criticism of government policies.

The Muslim Brotherhood also made important inroads into the labor community. Poor workers, who deeply resented their economic plight, eagerly listened to the stirring messages of the group. The circumstances of the Egyptian worker were in fact so shocking that even such outsiders as the British Embassy labor counselor were compelled to comment. In his words:

The Egyptian workers live in unhealthy and overcrowded dwellings— they are so overcrowded in many areas that the workers occupy the dwellings in shifts as in a factory; they sleep in the streets and in any odd corner; servants and their families sleep under staircases, in sheds and in gardens or in quarters in the more modern buildings which are often not sanitary. Their nutrition is usually inadequate and lacking in food values. Their health conditions are appalling and the provisions for dealing with diseases are totally inadequate. . . . There is no unemployment insurance, no provision for old age and similar state benefits.[17]

According to Richard Mitchell, whose work on the Brotherhood remains a classic,[18] Hasan al-Banna was ardent in his efforts to recruit workers. Evidently, al-Banna's interest was twofold: he wanted to save Islamic souls and also to protect Egyptian workers from the danger of foreigners or nonethnic Egyptians controlling the economy.

During the war and immediately after, labor support for the Brotherhood increased. Especially important for recruiting and maintaining a working-class membership was the labor section of the party. Workers were encouraged by the labor section to protest the government's inadequate handling of unemployment and its lack of concern for the economic problems of the poor. The labor section conducted economic research, engaged labor lawyers to defend the interests of mistreated workers, provided information about jobs, and even ran a labor school that educated workers about their rights under the law. Since the endorsement of labor was important to the Brotherhood, the party press devoted much attention to workers' issues—in particular, unemployment, the high cost of living, and the difficulties of life for the indigent.

The Muslim Brothers established labor unions—informed by fundamentalist ideas—among workers in the transport and textile industries of the big cities, in public utilities, and in some refineries in the Suez Canal area. By organizing workers, the Muslim Brothers attempted to weaken the force of the Wafdists and Communists in workers' affairs and demonstrate their commitment to wage earners. Through these unions, the Brotherhood had a direct influence on the strikes that occurred between 1946 and 1948.

Although trade unionism made great progress during the 1940s, the union movement only contained a minority of the work force and was most successful in organizing skilled male workers. Much of the working class, being illiterate, unskilled, and rural in origin, was occupied in small craft workshops that were seemingly immune to organization.

13. Village women traveling to Cairo

Women

In the latter decades of the nineteenth century, Muslim reformers in Egypt initiated a discussion on the role of women in society. Muhammad Abduh, and later such disciples as Qasim Amin and Ahmad Lutfi al-Sayyid, protested the status of women in the country and sought reform. These leaders were particularly concerned about laws unfavorable to women in matters of marriage, divorce, and polygamy, critical of the educational system that was discriminatory against girls, and opposed to the veiling of women and their social seclusion. Educated women were also writing about gender and the social situation in journals and magazines directed at female audiences.[19]

Even though some changes were taking place, men and women in general remained separated in both the private domain of the house and the more public sphere of the street during the first half of the twentieth century. The family was the nucleus of society, and most decisions were expected to derive from it. Marriages were still largely arranged, and women were regarded as legitimate possessions of men. Having limited input into or experience with the higher levels of government, education, business, or professional life, women on the whole did not exert a leadership role in public society. The inequality suffered by women was both legally and socially based. Although Islamic law allowed a woman to own property, carry out business, and inherit a portion of her father's estate equal to half her brother's share, the law put her at her husband's mercy in matters concerning divorce and the family.

The movement for expanding the role of women in society gained momentum as a result of the 1919 revolution when Egyptian women protested the British occupation and demonstrated in the streets alongside male family members. A few women were even jailed for short periods of time because of their political activities. Later, groups of "gentlewomen" began a social revolution when they threw off their veils, rejected the harem, and began to organize Egypt's social services.

14. Interior of the Muhammad Ali Mosque

Feminists trying to better the position of women in Egypt were from some of the most prominent families in the country. Huda Shaarawi, for example, who was closely allied with the Wafd, established the first Feminist Union in Egypt in 1923. Adopting a theme that was forwarded in the late nineteenth and early twentieth centuries, she and her colleagues argued that the cultural development of women was necessary for the enrichment of society. Their emphasis was on providing social welfare and easing the daily problems facing women—though their bias was in favor of the more affluent women.

Until World War II, the emancipation movement was confined to middle- and upper-class women with some education and exposure to Western ideas and did not have a mass following. With the dislocations of war, small but vocal groups of leftist and

Islamic-fundamentalist women were politicized and became increasingly interested in and articulate about the problems affecting female society. The women who joined the Communist underground were troubled by the relative absence of jobs for women, the poor salaries associated with female employment, the unequal system of education, and the prejudicial treatment women received even within the family. The fundamentalists were more concerned with trying to reconcile the changing social and gender roles with Quranic principles.

Women holding nontraditional political views did not join the mainstream feminist groups. Instead, the fundamentalists established the Muslim Sisters, whose goal was to educate women about Islam and the family's role as the core of society and to have an influence on how women conducted themselves both at home and in public. Secular feminists, especially at the university, were influenced by the Wafd and the Communist groups and maintained a continuous female presence in the student and nationalist movements until the 1952 revolution.

The idea of female emancipation touched a small minority of the Egyptian population—male or female—and could not depend on governmental support. But, especially since the 1940s, groups of women were becoming more outspoken, more critical, and more demanding. They continued to raise the issue of female rights, at the same time embracing wider political questions such as the national liberation of Egypt.

Conclusion

The rise of new social forces during the liberal age and the growing involvement of these forces in the political and economic life of the country represent important trends in modern Egyptian society. What is particularly noteworthy is the increasing distance that developed between these new groups and the political center. Initially, the Wafd engaged the popular classes with its nationalist rhetoric. But as the years passed and the

Wafd became less confrontational, much of the goodwill it had engendered was lost. Moreover, many clearly saw that Wafdist leaders used the popular classes for their own purposes in demonstrations and protests and gave the people little in return.

Unwittingly, the Wafd had provided alienated members of society with a model for protest. When the workers and the petty bourgeoisie used the very blueprint supplied by the Wafd in independent political action, or as "soldiers" in the Communist movement or the Muslim Brotherhood, they weakened the Wafd and any claim it had on popular sympathies.

[6]
Religion and Politics: The Battle of Conflicting Ideologies

Islam, Society, and Politics

Today, Islam is the religion of one-fifth of the world's population and the dominant faith in most of the Middle East. Islam requires its adherents to pray five times a day, to fast from sunup to sundown during the holy month of Ramadan, to make a pilgrimage to Mecca if health and circumstances allow, to give alms to the poor, and to profess their attachment to their faith. Islamic law has developed over time and has come to regulate many aspects of a believer's political, social, and private life. Islam has no formal clergy similar to that of the Christian priesthood. Prayer readers and religious leaders exist, but there is no intermediary between God and his servants.

Egypt is an Islamic country, and the overwhelming majority of its inhabitants are deeply attached to their faith. In acknowledgment of this, the Constitution of 1923 recognized Islam as Egypt's state religion. Religion has contributed significantly to modern Egypt's intellectual and political discourse and has also fundamentally shaped the attitudes of the majority of the Egyptian population. An analysis of the more important Islamic-oriented groups and trends in Egyptian society reveals the significant role religion has played as a guide for the faithful and also as a channel for the frustrations of the dispossessed.

The Ulema

The *ulema*, the learned men of Islam, have for centuries explained and commented on all matters of religion and law. As in other Islamic societies, the *ulema* in Egypt hold an honored place because of their association with the faith. Traditionally, the *ulema* have been socially conservative, politically anti-Western, and antisecular. Because their members offer judgments on a wide range of social and religious questions and expect compliance with their views from both leaders and the general population, the *ulema* appear to form an institution akin to a clergy. In theory, this is not the case; the *ulema* are not a priesthood and indeed have made no claims to mediate between man and God. In practice, however, the *ulema* have acquired the same social and religious authority and prestige (though not function) as the clergy in Christian communities.[1]

Yet as John Esposito notes in *Islam: The Straight Path*, the power and authority of the *ulema* have been reduced in the modern period.[2] Education, once the exclusive domain of this religious body, has been turned over to the state. Laws that in the past had been made by the *ulema* have become in the twentieth century the jurisdiction of civil lawyers, judges, and parliamentary officials. In the liberal age, especially, the *ulema* have had to face a progressively steady diminution of control as secular and constitutional forces have established a legal right to rule.

Muslim Reformers

Unlike the conservative *ulema* who sought no change in the legal, cultural, and social practices of society, a group of so-called Muslim reformers became active in Egypt in the late nineteenth century. Such notables as Shaykh Muhammad Abduh (1849–

1905) and Rashid Rida (1865–1935) were carrying on the tradition of Islamic renewal initiated by Jamal al-Din al-Afghani (1838–1897). These modernists believed in revitalizing the Islamic community in response to, and in recognition of, new conditions in the world. They were confident that the strength and flexibility of Islam would allow it to modernize. Arguing that Quranic law was not static, they maintained that it could be reinterpreted according to the needs of the day. Separating religious duties such as prayer, fasting, and the pilgrimage from social obligations recognized by criminal, civil, and family law, the modernists sought social and economic transformation within the formal structure of Islam. They suggested that although religious rules were unchanging, social conventions were open to modification. Muslim reformers were contrasting an inert Egyptian society with the impressive technological and industrial progress taking place in the Western world. They were also faced with local political and cultural leaders who were interested in advancing the causes of secularization and parliamentarianism. In consequence, Muslim reformers responded to the liberal age in different ways.

Muhammad Abduh, for instance, supported educational and legal reform, the emancipation of women, economic development, and governmental reorganization. Unlike al-Afghani, who was born in Iran and traveled throughout the Islamic world from Afghanistan to India, Iran, Egypt, and other parts of the Ottoman Empire, Muhammad Abduh was born in a village in the Egyptian delta to a family of some learning and piety.[3] He studied first at the Ahmadi Mosque in Tanta, a great center of Islamic thought, and later at al-Azhar, where he was particularly interested in logic, philosophy, and mystical theology.

Caught up in the nationalist spirit of the 1870s, Abduh and his mentor al-Afghani involved themselves in the Egyptian nationalist movement, a movement whose goal was to remove British and French influences from the country. For several years, Abduh's articles in the daily newspaper *al-Ahram* not only gave

15. Mosque of al-Azhar

voice to al-Afghani's political views but also expressed his own ideas. Through his journalistic activity, Abduh played a key role in forming public opinion on social and political matters and in enlightening the readership, especially on the need for quality national education. Not surprisingly, when the British occupied Egypt in 1882, they arrested, imprisoned, and ultimately exiled Abduh for three years. Abduh went to Paris where al-Afghani was staying. Together they organized a secret society and published a newspaper that pledged resistance to European expansionism through Islamic solidarity.[4]

After returning to Egypt in 1888, Abduh first became a judge in the court system and later Mufti of Egypt, putting him at the center of the country's system of Islamic law. As Mufti, Abduh committed himself to religious and educational reform and also continued his writihg. With his disciple Rashid Rida, he contributed to the periodical *al-Manar*, the organ of Islamic reform distilled through his own philosophical lens.

Muhammad Abduh fundamentally believed that the Islamic faith was compatible with modern thought and relevant to modern life. For him, no contradiction between Islam and the contemporary world existed, and to demonstrate this, Abduh insisted that social practices could be amended to reflect the specificity of the times. In particular, Abduh approved educational and legal reforms affecting the status of women and was critical of polygamy, which he recognized had an adverse affect on the family. Another of Abduh's disciples, Qasim Amin, expanded on his mentor's ideas about the status of women and gave the argument a more radical social orientation. In a book about women's emancipation that Amin published in 1899, he connected the deterioration of Islamic society with the breakdown of the family and concluded that women needed to be educated, employable, and respected, in order for progress to be realized. Amin maintained that Islam recognizes the equality of both sexes and protects women's rights. He disputed the argument that the Quran requires women to veil and seclude themselves and denounced polygamy and easy access to divorce (available to men). Amin did not, however, call for total parity between the sexes or for full participation of women in society since he did not suggest that they be granted political rights. Amin's book was widely debated and severely criticized by both religious and secular leaders who saw in his work traces of Western thought that they believed had no place in Islamic Egypt.

The Islamic modernist movement was important in Egypt. First, it attempted to lift the Islamic community out of a period of decline and reminded its members of Islam's past glory. Second, it joined in the movement for national independence, using Islam as the basis for strength and rejuvenation. Last, the discussion started by the modernists regarding Egypt's future development was continued by many Muslim activists following in their footsteps.

The Young Men's Muslim Association

Even after Britain granted Egypt nominal independence in 1922, a conspicuous foreign presence still remained in the country. This presence caused dissatisfaction, especially among young nationalists whose discontent was further exacerbated by an ineffectual domestic political leadership. Alienated from the mainstream of Egyptian political culture, some youth joined new organizations such as the Young Men's Muslim Association (YMMA), Young Egypt, and the Muslim Brotherhood, groups whose messages were informed by Islamic principles.

The YMMA was founded in Egypt in 1927 and spread throughout the Arab world. Though modeled on the structure of the Young Men's Christian Association (YMCA), the Muslim group was opposed to its sister organization, and in particular to the Christian missionary activity the YMCA countenanced. Based on an ideology of Pan-Islam, the YMMA was first and foremost a cultural, social, and religious organization. It developed extensive programs in entertainment and education and offered its members sports activities, drama classes, and adult instruction. Although separated from Wafdist nationalist politics by its own focus on Islam, the YMMA was not immune to the political movements and upheavals around it. The organization became a forum for nationalist activity and used a vocabulary infused with a militant Islamic content. Capturing a mostly young and middle-class student population, the YMMA filled a political and cultural gap that some members of this youthful generation acutely felt. Although the YMMA did not seek political power, the group did involve itself in the intellectual debates concerning Islam and modernization. The YMMA contributed to the ideological battle waged against Zionism in Egypt and the general wave of Islamization that occurred in the 1930s and 1940s.

Young Egypt

Young Egypt (Misr al-Fatat) was established in 1933 by the lawyer Ahmad Husayn. The organization sought the revitalization of Egypt's social and political life and in its early days recruited among secondary and university students in the major urban areas. Wearing the uniform of the paramilitary Green Shirts, the association's youthful members were often seen in the middle and late 1930s demonstrating in the streets and calling out slogans celebrating the glories of Egypt's past.

Young Egypt's prominence as an anti-Western organization grew during the 1930s when dissatisfaction with the Wafd and with liberal, secular democratic politics was on the rise. The rapid expansion in numbers that Young Egypt experienced suggested that young people were deeply disaffected and acutely eager to find an outlet for their frustrations and mounting anger. Because of this increasing numerical strength, Ahmad Husayn transformed the group into an official political party in 1938. Although emphasizing the revival of Egypt by the country's youth (who were called the soldiers of Egypt), the party tried to broaden its appeal, and indeed by the 1940s, urban lower- and middle-class adult males were counted among its adherents.

Young Egypt was a patriotic, militaristic, and socially conservative organization. In keeping with its Islamic orientation, Young Egypt stressed religion and morality as the guiding principles of life and consistently condemned corruption, decadence, the consumption of alcohol, and the relaxation of sexual mores. The party was both actively and philosophically opposed to the

European-style democracy practiced especially by the Wafd in Egypt and was allied ideologically to the Nazi and fascist groups active in Europe at the time.

Although party leaders looked back to past days of Islamic glory, they also focused on the material conditions of contemporary Egyptian society. They advocated industrial reform and agricultural change as prerequisites for development. For the countryside, the party proposed increasing the area of arable land and the level of production, establishing cooperative societies to aid and educate peasants, and extending agricultural credit. For industry, the party called for the establishment of an industrial bank, better tariff protections, and government regulations mandating the purchase of locally produced goods by state officials and students. Aware of the potential of an educated population, Young Egypt also favored free primary and low-cost secondary and university instruction, available to any Egyptians who wanted it. The party assigned to al-Azhar and its affiliated institutions the important task of building up Arabic and Islamic programs in Egypt and the Islamic world in an effort to revive interest in religious education.

When Young Egypt changed its name to the National Islamic party in 1940, its ideology became more radically religious and more conspicuously chauvinist. Among the newly formed directives to its members were the following commands: "Do not speak except in Arabic, and do not answer anyone who addresses you in a foreign language"; "Do not patronize commercial stores which do not carry Arabic signs"; "Do not buy anything except from an Egyptian, and do not wear clothes that are not produced in Egypt by Egyptians."[5]

Like its sometime friend, sometime rival, the Muslim Brotherhood, the National Islamic party sought to revolutionize Egypt politically, socially, and economically within the framework of Islamic theory and practice; violence was not ruled out as a tactic for the realization of nationalist goals. Despite such emotive slogans as "God, Fatherland, and King," and "Allah is Great, and

Glory belongs to Islam," the National Islamic party could not compete with the Muslim Brotherhood either in popularity or activity. Even after changing its name to the Socialist party before the 1952 revolution and stressing the twin themes of anti-imperialism and social reform, its activity was limited to that of a small opposition group.

Compared to the Muslim Brotherhood and the Communist movement, the party was sluggish after the war. But the organization was intact, and Ahmad Husayn's command was still effective. That effectiveness was shown in the role that the Socialist party played in the fire that devastated Cairo on January 26, 1952. From that day, the party has been accused (without convincing rebuttal) of burning down parts of the capital in an effort to undermine the rule of law in the country. Acting on behalf of the king, Husayn's militants allegedly made one last strike against parliamentary life in Egypt before drifting into historical obscurity.

The existence of Young Egypt, in large measure, signified the escalating disenchantment that sections of the population felt toward the secular establishment parties. Exhibiting Western modes of thought and process, the Wafd was criticized for not representing the mainstream of Egyptian public life.

The Muslim Brotherhood

The premier Islamic fundamentalist group in Egypt, the Muslim Brotherhood, was founded by Hasan al-Banna. Al-Banna was born in 1906 in the Delta province of al-Buhayra in the small town of al-Mahmudiyya. His father was a respected Islamic scholar and taught his son through Quranic study and personal practice to respect Islam. Al-Banna went to Cairo in the early 1920s to attend the teachers' college, Dar al-Ulum. There, he studied the ideas of the Islamic modernists, including the renowned Jamal al-Din al-Afghani and Muhammad Abduh. Also influenced by the more contemporary and indeed conservative thought of Rashid Rida, al-Banna was introduced to the concept of Islam as a self-sufficient ideology and convinced of the dangers of westernization.

Coming from a small town and a religious background, al-Banna was shocked by the highly secular and generally alien social, intellectual, and political trends he encountered in the capital. His early Cairene experience significantly influenced his thinking and prompted him to write in his memoirs: "Young men were lost, and the educated were in a state of doubt and confusion. . . . I saw that the social life of the beloved Egyptian nation was oscillating between her dear and precious Islamism which she had inherited, defended, lived with and become accustomed to, and made powerful during thirteen centuries, and this severe Western invasion which is armed and equipped with all the destructive and degenerative influences of money, wealth, prestige, ostentation, material enjoyment, power, and means of propaganda."[6] Al-Banna was coming to believe that all of Egypt's problems were traceable to westernization and the unfortunate departure from fundamental Islam.

In 1927, al-Banna went to Ismailiyya in the Suez Canal Zone to teach in a government primary school. In and around Ismailiyya, al-Banna came into contact with British soldiers stationed at the local base and French officials employed by the Suez Canal Company. Deeply offended by the very presence of foreigners, and dedicated to radical nationalist ideas and religious practices, he established the Muslim Brotherhood in 1928. The organization first took the form of an Islamic revivalist movement. In a short time, the group developed a political orientation that was antagonistic to the secular parties dominating the political arena and directly opposed to European-style government and Western standards of behavior. Al-Banna promoted a simple and absolute message to his followers: struggle to rid Egypt of foreign occupation; defend and obey Islam. According to the new association, Islam was not simply a matter of individual piety or an aspect of social and political life. Rather, Islam was a comprehensive ideology that embraced both the personal and public arenas and provided the foundation for Islamic state and society.[7]

Al-Banna, who took the title of supreme guide, adopted a literal interpretation of the Quran. For him, Islam's principles and commandments regulated all matters of life for every Muslim in every age and in every community. According to al-Banna, Islam was universal, ageless, and comprehensive and should be observed meticulously. Al-Banna's dream was to impose Islam on every aspect of life in Egypt—social, political, intellectual, and personal. He believed that through Islam the country could be rejuvenated and the people returned to their most natural and innocent state.

From the beginning, the Muslim Brotherhood was active in the field of education. It established primary and secondary schools for boys and girls and technical schools for workers; it offered courses explaining the Quran and classes teaching basic skills to the illiterate. In keeping with the philosophical teachings of the organization, a distinct Islamic character was built into all the organization's programs. Also committed to appropriate social and economic reform in Egypt, the organization generated urban projects that provided jobs for the poor and the unemployed. The Brotherhood set up industrial and commercial enterprises that while helping the indigent also created economic strength for the organization and undermined the non-Islamic entrepreneurs active in the country.

Especially after al-Banna relocated to Cairo in the early 1930s, the organization became more Pan-Islamic and more visible. Subsequently, the number of militants within it increased. Although the newest members of the Brotherhood were particularly receptive to its religious missionary activity, the general economic distress caused by the 1929 depression contributed to the organization's increasing popularity. By the outbreak of World War II, the Brotherhood counted among its members civil servants, students, workers, policemen, lawyers, soldiers, and peasants, and the movement's strength was variously estimated at somewhere from many hundreds of thousands to beyond a million activists. Although the rural members were vital to the organization, the urban activists, representing an emergent and self-conscious Muslim middle class, shaped policy and determined strategy.

The Brotherhood was an extraparliamentary organization that exerted a considerable influence on lower- and middle-class members of Egyptian society. This influence was especially evident in the countless demonstrations, marches, and protests the Brotherhood staged between 1945 and 1948, the period when the movement was strongest. During these years, the organization also acted on the instructions of various ruling governments, as a counterweight to the Communists and Wafdists. Opposed both to the secular bases of Communist and Wafdist ideologies and to the democratic, constitutional, and cosmopolitan society they envisioned, the Brotherhood would sabotage meetings, precipitate clashes at public gatherings, and even damage property. This behavior was characteristic of the Brotherhood in the years after the war, when the terrorist tactics it increasingly employed brought fear and disruption to Egyptian society. Accused of carrying out many of the political assassinations that took place in Egypt in the 1940s, the Brotherhood advocated a militancy that went far beyond the imaginations of Egypt's established political leaders.

Of all the causes embraced by the Brotherhood in the 1940s, the struggle in Palestine was among the most passionate. The organization argued in numerous newspaper articles devoted to the subject that Arab Palestine must be safeguarded against a European-Zionist takeover. Furthermore, it insisted that Palestine's Islamic heritage be protected and in particular Jerusalem's shrines secured. The Brotherhood collected money and arms, trained volunteers, and sent a battalion of troops to Palestine in 1948 to join the Arab forces there.

Not a localized conflict, the war in Palestine caused political tensions to soar in Egypt. In particular, the Brotherhood undertook a series of limited attacks against Egyptian Jews that the palace did nothing to halt. The king, moreover, launched an anti-Marxist campaign against the Egyptian Communist movement (which was incorrectly accused of being Zionist) after it supported the partition of Palestine. Amidst the deterioration of parliamentary life, Prime Minister Mahmud al-Nuqrashi imposed martial law and using the power available to him outlawed the Brotherhood in December 1948. He considered this justifiable punishment for an organization that plotted revolution against the state and carried out relentless terrorist attacks against individuals.

In retaliation, al-Nuqrashi himself was assassinated by an angry member of the Brotherhood. Leaders of the political mainstream, enraged and exasperated by the continued violence of the Brotherhood, sought revenge. This time, al-Banna lost his life. He was murdered by the political police, with the order very likely coming from the government and being approved by the palace.[8]

The movement then went underground for several years and was much weakened by the loss of its charismatic and energetic leader. In the spring of 1951, the Brotherhood was temporarily allowed to resume limited activity in the more open environment following the Wafd's reinstatement to power. The group was supposedly restricted to cultural, social, and spiritual services and not allowed either to engage in political work or to sustain military units. This restriction was not, however, honored. The Brotherhood took part in the guerrilla war being fought in the Suez Canal Zone against the continued British presence. Given the general disintegration of political life, the government could not control the situation, and the Brotherhood continued its military attacks on the British with relative impunity.

Under the leadership of its new supreme guide, Shaykh Hasan Ismail al-Hudaybi, the Brotherhood attempted to continue its activity. But when it clashed in 1954 with the military government of Gamal Abdul Nasser, the organization was banned, and many of its members were imprisoned and tortured. During the 1950s, the movement could not regain the prominence nor recover the membership of the days of Hasan al-Banna. The legacy of the Muslim Brotherhood, however, as articulated by Hasan al-Banna and the organization's chief ideologue Sayyid Qutb, is an important one not only in Egypt but also in other Middle Eastern countries, such as Syria, Kuwait, Jordan, and the Sudan, where offshoots of the organization emerged and where the ideology of neorevivalism spread.

John Esposito has eloquently pointed out that the ideology of the neorevivalists was deeply appealing to a broad base of people and rooted in a number of important factors.[9] Essential was the neorevivalists' indigenous analysis of religion and society. Unlike al-Afghani, Muhammad Abduh, and the Islamic modernists of the early decades of the twentieth century, the Muslim Brothers never discussed the compatibility of Islam with the West. In contrast, al-Banna and Qutb both shunned the West, convinced that Islam alone was able to address the complexity of modern issues and find answers to modern problems. It was equally significant that neorevivalism was based on mass activism, which involved increasing numbers of people and demanded that they be loyal, disciplined, and highly trained. Whether engaged in religious instruction, journalistic activity, hospital care, industrial enterprise, or social-welfare projects, a new group of people was being groomed to lead the future Islamic society. Finally, the neorevivalism of the Brotherhood struck a moral and social chord among the traditional sectors of the population, who were disappointed with the earthly doctrines of capitalism, liberal democracy, secularism, and Marxism and who (like the Brotherhood itself) denounced such vices as the commingling of the sexes, the drinking of alcohol, and the imitation of Western dress.

The Muslim Brotherhood encouraged people in the 1930s, 1940s, and 1950s to see in Islam an answer to the problems of the modern age. But the group's organizational importance and its ideological relevance have also been visible in the more recent decades of the 1970s and 1980s, as the militancy of Islamic fundamentalism has lately demonstrated.

The Egyptian Communist Movement

After the Egyptian Communist party was crushed in the mid-1920s, a Marxist movement ceased to exist until the late 1930s.[10] When oppositional activity was renewed at this time, it occurred in a relatively free political arena. The Constitution, which the antiparliamentarian prime minister Ismail Sidqi had abrogated in 1930, was restored in 1935, and political life became lively once more. The Wafd was revitalized and activated. The Muslim Brotherhood and Young Egypt were energized and began organizing their paramilitary forces. Liberals and democrats, many of whom were from Egypt's Jewish community, openly expressed antifascist sentiments and then revived Marxist thinking in the country. Such Western-oriented, cosmopolitan Egyptians served as conduits of Western radical ideology to indigenous Egyptians.

The cosmopolitan community was schooled in Western languages. Its members read foreign newspapers, listened to foreign radio broadcasts, and were familiar with the encroachment of the fascist campaign. The exposure to Western culture through language should not be underestimated. Literate in at least French and English, many of Egypt's intellectual Jews were conversant with Enlightenment philosophy and aware of the ideas and movements current abroad.

Cosmopolitan Egyptians, and primarily young Jews, set up clubs with a political, cultural, or intellectual content; Egyptian Muslims and Copts participated but to a much lesser extent. These clubs became centers of dissidence, where like-minded people met, exchanged ideas, and learned more about the world in which they lived. In this context, issues of the day were studied, lectures given, books recommended, and thoughts clarified, giving a political and social education to youth favorably predisposed to the left.

The efforts of Jewish students and intellectuals to become involved in the political process in Egypt reflected their desire to understand the dynamics of the international situation—particularly the rise of fascism in Europe and the political divisions of right and left. Amid international aggression and the threat to their own community, Jews were trying to locate a place for themselves in an unsettled and increasingly hostile world. Moving from antifascism to Marxism then became something of a natural progression for some of the Jewish activists. They were stimulated by the socialist ideas being imported from Europe, enraged by the continued British occupation, horrified by nazism and the brutality of World War II, and deeply affected by the misery and injustice suffered by the mass of the population. When in the early 1940s they created the clandestine Communist movement, they were expressing a political as well as a national need. Not only were they disenchanted with mainstream politics in Egypt, which had failed to win independence or improve the quality of life, but they also wanted more direct participation in Egyptian national affairs. It is possible that Jews advocated an internationalist ideology like Marxism because it was a way for them to build into the majority culture; it was a path toward self-identification with the larger society.[11] By condemning narrow ethnic sectarianism and stressing the importance of social class, Jews felt for the first time that they could participate in Egypt's political life and find a place for themselves in a society in which they were a small and isolated minority.

The history of Egyptian communism from World War II is the the history of factionalism and dissension. No single, recognized Communist party existed. Instead, when Marxist militants launched their formal activity in the early 1940s, they established a number of different, sometimes mutually hostile, organizations. The most important groups were the Egyptian Movement for National Liberation (EMNL), Iskra, and the New Dawn. After the nationalist movement gained momentum in 1947, a partial, but only temporary, unification in the Marxist movement occurred and produced the Democratic Movement for National Liberation

(DMNL). A discussion of these groups within the context of Egyptian politics follows.

The Egyptian Movement for National Liberation

The EMNL was the most dynamic of the Communist organizations and advocated the immediate proletarianization and Egyptianization of its membership. The group concentrated its efforts on attempting to build a truly popular organization by recruiting Nubians and Sudanese, Egyptian aviation and textile workers, the petty bourgeoisie, and the poor of al-Azhar. Its leader, Henri Curiel, maintained that a party lived not on the grand issues but rather on the mundane ones, that is, on the specific struggles of workers, peasants, and civil servants. Curiel hoped to organize villagers, the urban poor, military men, and trade unionists. Although he was at best only moderately successful, that the EMNL could recruit militants into the revolutionary underground reflected the heterogeneity of political commitments in this period.

Curiel was an interesting figure.[12] He was born into a rich Jewish-Egyptian family in 1914. His father was a banker, businessman, and landowner. Curiel received a European education, first at the Jesuit school in Cairo and later at the École Française de Droit where he received a bachelor of arts degree in law. When Curiel reached the age of twenty-one, he took Egyptian nationality, relinquishing the right to his father's Italian passport and thereby eschewing the privileges of foreign citizenship. Given his background, he was an unlikely Communist; yet, he was the most important figure in the movement until 1950 when he was arrested and then deported from the country. He never returned to Egypt.

Deeply touched by both the Egyptian nationalist movement and the condition of life prevailing in the country, Curiel began reading Marxist texts soon after the signing of the Anglo-Egyptian Treaty in 1936 in the hope of finding answers to Egypt's nagging problems. Paradoxically perhaps as a beneficiary of

Egypt's class system, Curiel was acutely aware of the contradictions inherent in a society where the vast majority lived in wretched poverty while a tiny minority enjoyed excessive wealth. The elders of the Jewish community, dismayed by his outspoken attitudes and controversial behavior, considered him reckless for voluntarily involving himself in local politics. Disregarding their warnings, he became active in a campaign that led him on a collision course with the police, his family, and the political establishment.

When Curiel began trying to understand how to build a party, he tried to meet the survivors of the first Egyptian Communist party. From the old-timers he learned that although the cadres were full of goodwill, they were easily destroyed because they were set up by Soviet agents, they had no coherent party structure, and the members had little theoretical knowledge and no notion of how a cell functioned.[13] Curiel feared that launching a party too quickly without a strong base to support it would cause it to fall as rapidly as the first Egyptian Communist party had fallen. Instead, Curiel opted to move slowly, and he and his followers adopted "the line of the democratic forces" that essentially called for the formation of a united national front, bringing together all leftist forces including the petty bourgeoisie, the national bourgeoisie, workers, and peasants.

Concentrating on the issues of national independence, class inequality, and the status of the Sudan, the EMNL tried to politicize an increasing number of disenchanted people and provide an alternative to the mainstream political parties, which had failed to address satisfactorily the multitude of social, political, and economic problems facing the country.

Iskra

The second most important Communist group was Iskra, founded by Hillel Schwartz. Unlike the EMNL, Iskra had an essentially Jewish leadership and was composed of members who were bourgeois in social origin, thinking, and life-style. Many of the members in fact spoke little or no Arabic, using

French at home, at school, and in social discourse. A few years after it was established, the group began recruiting into its ranks Egyptian Muslims from well-to-do, intellectual families. Many of Iskra's members were students and intellectuals from Cairo University where Iskra became the largest Communist group and was particularly well represented in the faculties of the liberal arts and scientific professions.

To accommodate Iskra's theoretical orientation, Hillel Schwartz outlined the stages theory of organization that was adopted as a way of circumventing the built-in difficulties of having upper-class and minority Egyptians recruit local workers into the underground movement. His system worked in the following way: First, radical minorities—especially Jews—were brought into the group; next, sympathetic Egyptian intellectuals were recruited. These two groups shared a common social background, lifestyle, and education. According to the plan, the indigenous Egyptian cadres, who could speak Arabic and better relate to workers, were to politicize members of the working class in an effort to build a future proletarian party. Although Egyptian intellectuals joined Iskra, few workers were members.

The basic program of Iskra was similar to that of the EMNL, as one of Iskra's participants noted: "If you take the political lines of the two movements and the slogans that were raised, I don't think you could distinguish at least on the surface, any big difference. I think that the differences were in how these political lines were interpreted and implemented. . . . There was a difference in social constitution and in the degree of fusion with the national movement—to which the EMNL was closer. There was a difference, therefore, in the way all problems were looked at. . . . The words were the same but what was put inside by each group was different."[14]

The New Dawn

The New Dawn, the third Communist group worthy of note, was set up to study and understand Egyptian society and to develop a Communist policy specific to the particular characteristics of the country. The group's aim was to establish relations in the Egyptian nationalist and trade-union movements, and it was somewhat successful in organizing Cairene and Alexandrian factories and in developing a lasting influence in working-class circles. Although the working class was considered to have the vanguard role in the nationalist struggle, New Dawn's leaders believed that the creation of a conventional Communist party during World War II was premature. The organization was small, membership numbering only in the hundreds, but was responsible for carrying forward important oppositional ideas through its commitment to journalism and its constant defense of workers' rights.

Leaders of the organization published the serious and influential magazine *al-Fajr al-Jadid* (the New Dawn) that reported on a variety of issues including foreign control over the Egyptian economy, imperialism, democracy, and education. The magazine defended Arab unity and contributed to laying the foundations of a new school in art and poetry in Egypt.

Its leaders were also disproportionately Jewish and middle class.

The Democratic Movement for National Liberation— An Attempt at Unification

The Communist organizations were highly nationalist and critical of Egypt's traditional political culture. Formal militant activity took place in small, autonomous, clandestine groups limited to close associates and friends. Because no single, unified Communist party existed, Communist activity in the 1940s was prone to extreme divisiveness. Born outside of the framework of the Egyptian political system, the movement developed apart from free and open political discourse. The margin in which it was forced to operate was defined by state law and narrowed by its own subterranean practices. The movement could not grow through the interchange—either hostile or friendly—so common in lawful political activity. In consequence, each group that was established became highly suspicious of the intentions, aspirations, and goals of presumably antagonistic competitors, those who in fact had been former allies in the antifascist movement. Insecurity and skepticism separated the leftists and shaped the content of the clandestine organizations. Since there was no experience at the beginning of the movement with internal party struggle, the idea of banding together with others holding even slightly divergent ideological or organizational views was considered opportunism. Thus, instead of forming a united Communist organization with admittedly diverse elements committed to working out their differences within a corporate structure, the Communist movement began divided and remained for most of its life under the monarchy fractious and dismembered.

The Communist movement was compelled to confront its factionalism and indeed reevaluate its policies and performance as a result of the concerted nationalist activity, in the form of spontaneous popular demonstrations, strikes, and protests, that erupted across Egypt between February 9 and March 4, 1946. Demands for independence, current since the early days of Saad Zaghlul, were repeated but were infused with new expectations and possibilities. Egyptians expected a commitment to evacuate from the British in return for the supportive role their nation had played during the war. Eventually, British withdrawal became an urgent demand supported by a wide cross section of the Egyptian populace.

Prior to the nationalist upheaval, the sectarian squabbling among the predominantly upper-class and cosmopolitan intellectuals who formed the Communist movement was of largely academic interest. Once the masses became politicized around the cause of nationalism, however, the division of the left had enormous practical implications. Almost against their will, the leftist leaders had to submerge their ideological differences if they were—through unity—to play a role in shaping the course of the nationalist struggle. In 1947, the Democratic Movement for National Liberation (DMNL) was created out of the EMNL and

Iskra. The Communist movement, however, continued to suffer from dissension, personality clashes, and police strikes against it. Although the nationalist movement brought the divergent Communist trends together, they could not coexist for long. Soon after unity was accomplished, dozens of organizations, offshoots of the DMNL, appeared on the political scene, most of them transiently. Because the DMNL did not tolerate dialogue or disagreement within the organization, differences of opinion resulted in expulsion or resignation rather than compromise or discussion, causing factionalism to accelerate.

By the end of the 1940s, the Communist movement was weak, divided, and isolated from the people it hoped to represent. Recruiting greater numbers of Coptic and Muslim Egyptians into the movement and promoting them into leadership positions had not improved the situation. A temporary turnabout came, however, at the beginning of the 1950s when there was a dramatic improvement in the spirits, expectations, and activities of the members of the Communist underground. This reversal was to a large extent brought about by the return of the Wafd party to power in January 1950 in the last truly free general election in Egypt's modern political history, by the release of numerous political prisoners from the camps and prisons, and by a more open political atmosphere.

Once again, conditions became ripe for renewed political activity. The nationalist and anticolonialist movements were reinforced, the university campuses were alive with political militancy, workers' strikes multiplied throughout the country, and the peace movement rallied. Communists, responding to this activity, were again building up their forces in an effort to capture at least some of the vitality of the popular movements.

When the anti-British guerrilla activity (in which the Communists participated) occurred in 1951 and 1952 in the Suez Canal Zone, a popularist challenge was leveled not only against the colonizers but also against the Egyptian political elites who had over time proved impotent with respect to the British. The Wafd, historically in control of the nationalist movement, had by now lost control. People were impatient with the whole structure of Egyptian politics—with the king, the conventional parties, and the existing institutions. They were ready for major change in the country. Many believed that the Communists or the Islamic fundamentalists would be the natural heirs to political power in Egypt; each group was organized, politically conscious, and gaining in popularity. However, because neither group was actually set up to take power, neither captured the moment.

The Emergence of a New Group—The Egyptian Communist Party

Even the appearance of a new group in 1949, the Egyptian Communist party (ECP), which satisfied some of the disgruntled members of the DMNL could not solve the problems that strained and weakened the Marxist movement. Instead, the ECP's leader, Fuad Mursi, set out to analyze Egyptian society and provide appropriate political principles on which to build a disciplined political organization. Mursi categorized Egypt as a semifeudal, semicolonized country where the immediate battle to be waged was the national democratic revolution against imperialist domination of the country. The working class, the peasants, and the progressive intellectuals were targeted as the forces of the revolution. Large landowners, capitalists of foreign origin, and the national bourgeoisie were considered traitorous to national liberation.

The leaders of the ECP hoped that the establishment of the new organization would end the chronic divisions within the Marxist movement. However, their competitors, generally from the DMNL, argued that by founding another group the disunity of the movement was further perpetuated. Moreover, these critics asserted that since two of the important leaders of the group, Fuad Mursi and Ismail Sabri Abd Allah, were studying in Paris from the mid-1940s until 1949–1950, they had not even been present in Egypt when the nationalist movement was vibrant and when nationalist ferment led to the partial unity of the Communist movement. According to Communists who had been operating in Egypt for years, the leaders of the ECP ignored previous efforts to radicalize society and belittled the limited victories Marxists had achieved during the past decade. The ECP leadership was criticized for acting as though it was creating a new Communist movement in Egypt, using nothing that had existed previously. This, of course, angered a significant portion of the movement.

The Significance of the Communists

In the end, the Communists never managed to diffuse their ideas widely. They were unable to move out of the political center of Cairo and outside of the social strata of urban students, professionals, and skilled workers. Despite some efforts, Communists with few exceptions could not penetrate the rural villages or the poor urban neighborhoods. The Communists did not transform their message of popular participation in the political process into concrete activity.

But despite the movement's difficulties, Egyptian communism had a surprisingly enduring presence. It faced and withstood factionalism, police repression, ideological confusion, and numerical weakness. In the 1940s and 1950s, it constituted an oppositional force worthy of note because of its influence on Egyptian intellectual and political life, an influence achieved primarily through its contributions to journalism, poetry, short-story writing, and philosophical and political publications and through demonstrations and strikes. The Communists were present at key moments of nationalist, student, and trade-union militancy. Whether in the streets protesting political corruption, in the schools and universities debating their vision of a new future, or in the trade unions demanding basic reforms, the Communists gave voice to the dissatisfactions and disappointments of the population at large.

Moreover, the Communists helped lay the basis for left-wing ideas—social justice, planned economic development, and skepticism of the West—that became a basic part of the political, social, intellectual, and artistic mainstream of Egypt under Nasser's rule. The Communists also contributed to the ultimate destabilization of the constitutional monarchy in Egypt. By criticizing the Wafd and questioning its commitment to independence and modernization, by attacking the king and his political associates, and by charging that members of the minority parties acted as obstacles to change, the Communists helped create an ideological climate in which the Free Officers could organize and operate. Indeed, the Communist campaign to discredit the activities and aspirations of the mainstream parties helped pave the way for the emergence of Gamal Abdul Nasser and his military partners.

[7]
Cultural Expression in Egypt

During the thirty-year period between independence (1922) and revolution (1952), a diverse and ever-widening political culture developed. Intellectual diversity, which would become almost unknown in the following decades, expanded horizons and encouraged discussion of Egypt's identity, its colonial status, and its place in the international arena. Intellectuals wrestled with the themes of nationalism, Islam, and pharaonism. In addition, an imported European literary and classical tradition informed some of the writings published during Egypt's liberal age.

A striking feature of this burgeoning political culture was the relative openness of Egyptian intellectual life, as seen in the variety of philosophical and cultural ideas that were expressed in novels, plays, essays, and especially newspaper articles. The periodical press in Egypt, from as far back as the late nineteenth century, played an important role in diffusing modern ideas and experiences by covering a range of topics from international affairs to scientific and literary developments. Egyptian journalism owes a great debt to immigrants from Greater Syria, who came to Egypt after the 1860s and were largely responsible for establishing the medium in Egypt. *Al Ahram*, *al-Muqtataf*, and *al-Hilal*, for example, were all founded by journalists from Lebanon. Shielded from the strict censorship imposed on the territories of Greater Syria by the sultan in Constantinople, Egypt was a freer and more open environment in which to work in the late nineteenth century.

Indigenous Egyptians did not become active in the field of journalism until after World War I, when they began publishing such notable papers as *al-Wafd al Misri, Roz al-Yusuf,* and *al-Kutla.* In the 1930s and 1940s, the nonparliamentary, nonmainstream political organizations established newspapers as a method of outreach; the Muslim Brotherhood published an organ, and leftist groups issued a variety of publications. Although the lesser periodicals of the time provided a legal platform for controversial and dissident ideas, the Egyptian press in general offered writers a forum for testing out new forms of prose and poetry. This was especially important for young writers who had no other outlet for their ideas.

Even though the Egyptian reading public was small in the first half of the twentieth century, Egypt's high intellectuals produced outstanding work in literature, history, and philosophy. Many intellectuals were conversant with Western culture and values and also schooled in Arabic and Islamic literature. They read widely in a number of traditions and languages and were highly sophisticated. Through their research and writings, they endeavored to understand their own society, develop a local culture, and engage fellow intellectuals in a national debate on diverse social, national, and religious questions.

Many among Egypt's high intelligentsia were strongly oriented toward French or English culture. Taha Husayn, Muhammad Husayn Haykal, Tawfiq al-Hakim, Ahmad Amin, Abbas Mahmud al-Aqqad, and Ibrahim Abd al-Qadir al-Mazini,[1] for example, were influenced by European intellectual and political traditions and tended to embrace liberalism in its broadest sense. By publicizing these Western ideas, even if among the intellectual elite, these writers helped create the culture of liberalism that existed in Egypt for three decades. Because they supported national independence and constitutionalism and respected individual rights, equality for women, and universal education, these ideas and causes became respectable and acceptable to an increasingly wide audience. In magazine articles, books, novels, and plays, these writers expressed their thoughts, revealed their hopes, and voiced their disillusionment. Although they often spoke only to one another, they also spoke for the less articulate who found neither the written words nor the cultural forums to communicate nationalist or religious sentiments.

Writers and Their Work

Taha Husayn (1889–1973) was born in a small town in Upper Egypt into a family of very modest means. Illness at a young age left him blind. After a traditional early education, he attended Cairo University and then spent four years at the Sorbonne. After his return to Egypt in 1919, he was at the center of intellectual life in the country as a teacher, administrator, literary editor, novelist, and essayist. In 1926, Husayn became the subject of a controversy with the publication of his book *On Pre-Islamic Poetry*. The work, and the author, were publicly condemned by religious leaders for betraying accepted Islamic dogma. The scandal involved Husayn's interpretation of pre-Islamic poetry, poetry that had conventionally been considered a linguistic reference source for interpreting the Quran. According to Husayn's study, however, "this poetry proves nothing and tells us nothing and should not be used, as it has been, as an instrument in the science of the Quran and the Hadith."[2]

Husayn's book affronted the religious establishment and was seen as endangering traditionalism in a number of ways. First, because the author denied that the poetry had in fact been written before the rise of Islam, he refuted the idea that it could serve as a basis for interpreting the Quran. Second, he challenged the integrity of Muslim authorities themselves. Third, he argued in favor of the introduction of secularism into literary criticism and extolled the virtues of Cartesian rational philosophy. The outcry against the book was immediate and dramatic. Conservative *ulema* led by Rashid Rida of *al-Manar* newspaper decried Husayn's irreverent methodology and conclusions and demanded, unsuccessfully, that he be dismissed from his post as dean of the Faculty of Arts at Cairo University.

Taha Husayn was not, however, the first modern writer to defy the religious community. In 1925, Shaykh Ali Abd al-Raziq (1888–1966), a liberal who belonged to one of Egypt's great landed families, published a book entitled *Islam and the Principles of Political Authority*. His tract, which was also condemned by the religious establishment, profoundly affected his professional life. Because of its publication, he was dismissed from his post as judge in the Sharia Court of Mansura and expelled from the ranks of the *ulema*.

Abd al-Raziq wrote about the caliphate[3] and reiterated the position, first put forward by Mustafa Kemal in Turkey, that the caliphate should be abolished since it was not a necessary institution in Islam. (Kemal did put an end to the caliphate in 1924.) According to Abd al-Raziq's reading of history, the first four successors of Muhammad legitimately held the title of caliph; such was not the case with those who followed. Often, argued Abd al-Raziq, political or military might boosted otherwise objectionable men to the position of head of state, compromising the significance of the office and distorting its historical place in Islam.

It was Abd al-Raziq's view that since no particular system of government was stipulated by the Prophet, the form of rule chosen should simply reflect the requirements of the times. If a caliph were to assume power in the modern era, he would have to be *chosen* by the Islamic people, for the people possess sovereignty. For Abd al-Raziq, a constitutional government with checks on the absolutist control of the monarch—in this case King Fuad—was particularly preferable to a caliph. Abd al-Raziq felt that although a constitution would guarantee to serve the people, a caliph could easily become authoritarian and concern himself only with the maintenance of his own power.

Neither Abd al-Raziq nor Taha Husayn were lone voices; each had a section of the mainstream political community behind him.

The former was supported by the Liberal Constitutionalists, the latter by the Wafdists. Both questioned the appropriateness of traditional values in the modern world and by implication opened a debate on the legitimacy of absolutist control.

Taha Husayn, the more famous and the more prolific, published an impressive range of works. His memoirs, for instance, have been widely read in Egypt and abroad; his novels, *Adib* and *The Call of the Karawan*, have received considerable attention in the Arab world; and his analytical works have helped to deepen intellectual discourse in the country. His three-volume work entitled *On the Margin of the Prophet's Way of Life, Ala hamish al-sira* (1937–1943), received widespread attention because it was devoted to fictionalized stories of Muhammad's life. This work was published during a period when increased attention was being paid to religious subjects by a variety of secular Egyptian intellectuals. Islamic works, ranging from apologetic literature to analyses of serious theological questions, were published at a remarkable rate during the 1930s. Apparently, the reading audience appreciated the move to religious themes and encouraged the authors by endorsing their work.

Unlike his highly controversial early writings, Husayn's later works reflected the traditional authorities' view of Islam and the Prophet and thus represented a departure from his once unqualified commitment to reason. Some critics viewed Husayn's religious books as a complete retreat from his adherence to rationalism. Those critics more sympathetic toward the writer believed that he simply carried forward his view of Islam by communicating the essence of the faith in new ways that were more appropriate to the modern Egyptian consciousness.

Although he was writing about the Prophet and early Islam, Taha Husayn was also thinking of other, very different, kinds of subjects. In 1938, for example, just two years after the signing of the Anglo-Egyptian Treaty, Husayn published one of his more important books, *The Future of Culture in Egypt*. The timing was significant because during the first years after the treaty, Husayn was particularly optimistic about Egypt's future: "I felt, as other Egyptians did . . . that Egypt was beginning a new period of her life: she had obtained some of her rights, and must now set herself to important duties and heavy responsibilities. . . . We live in an age which can be defined as one in which freedom and independence are not an end to which peoples and nations strive, but a means to ends higher, more permanent, and more comprehensive in their benefits."[4] Now that Egypt was truly independent, according to Husayn, its leaders could revitalize the country and thus improve the quality of national life, operate an energetic democracy, and assure civic liberties for all citizens.

The Future of Culture in Egypt was written in two parts. In the first section, Husayn considered the significance of modern Europe and located Egypt's place within the sphere of Western culture. In his view, to be modern and to be civilized was to be European. He argued that "so far has the European ideal become our ideal that we now measure the material progress of all individuals and groups by the amount of borrowing from Europe."[5] Husayn was so convinced of Egypt's need to associate itself with the West that he wrote: "In order to become equal partners in civilization with the Europeans, we must literally and forthrightly do everything that they do; we must share with them the present civilization with all its pleasant and unpleasant sides, and not content ourselves with words and mere gestures. Whoever advises another course is a deceiver or is himself deceived."[6]

The book's second section included a discussion of Egypt's educational system and recommended widespread reform: the unification of the school system, an updated curriculum, and the establishment of universal education. Al-Azhar was to be revamped according to the standards of secular institutions.

Taha Husayn, like others of his generation, was trying to understand Egypt's history and the country's place in the world. His contemporary, Ahmad Amin (1886–1954), was also deeply influenced by the ideas of liberalism and wrote about the relationship between Egypt and the West in his widely circulated book *Orient and Occident*. Amin respected much about the West: its commitment to constitutionalism, individual rights, and universal education; technical and scientific achievement; rationality; and national independence. But he was also critical of the West's materialism, lack of spirituality, and arrogance. Unlike Husayn who located Egypt in Mediterranean culture, Amin believed that Egypt fit squarely in the East, and he credited the East with spiritual qualities and ethical teachings that were higher than those practiced in the West.

Another contemporary, Muhammad Husayn Haykal (1889–1956), was born in the same year as Taha Husayn, but into a family of affluent landowners with important political connections. Haykal first studied law at Cairo University and then went to Paris where he earned a doctorate. While studying in Paris, Haykal wrote what is considered to be the first purely Egyptian novel, *Zaynab*, a story about life in the Egyptian countryside. The work was originally published anonymously in Egypt, but after it was highly praised, Haykal happily claimed it as his own. Haykal authored many books and articles about Egypt and was also intimately involved in politics.

He was among the founders of the Liberal Constitutionalist party and edited its newspaper, *al-Siyasa*. He held the ranks of minister of state and minister of education in various cabinets, took over as party leader when Muhammad Mahmud died in 1941, and led the Liberal Constitutionalists into the coalition government that presided over Egypt in the 1940s. During that time, he was president of the Senate.

Among Haykal's many interests was language and, in particular, the Arabic language's ability to express the thoughts of modern civilization. His efforts to refine the language, which appeared in countless articles in *al-Siyasa*, were geared toward the formation of a national culture, a culture aware of the West but not a replication of it. Like his contemporaries, he published a series of books on religious topics—in particular, the life of the Prophet and the first four caliphs. In the 1930s when he was wrestling with political, historical, and religious questions, Haykal essentially abandoned his commitment to the liberal values inherent in Western civilization and instead stressed the intellectual and ethical content of early Islam. Reason and science, once hailed as among the hallmarks of Western culture, were now dubbed as tools insufficient for the happiness of man. Haykal attacked the West, rejected much of European culture, and apologetically offered Islam as the best answer to modern problems.

An associate of Husayn and Haykal, Tawfiq al-Hakim was also French educated and cultured. He was trained in law both in Cairo and in Paris and was expected by his family to pursue a legal career. Al-Hakim, however, became more interested in literature and the theater than in advocacy and devoted himself to a career in writing plays, several novels, stories, and essays.

Political events inspired al-Hakim's literary and philosophical works and prompted his belief that Egypt was rousing itself from years of cultural slumber. The 1919 revolution, the limited independence of 1922, and the Constitution of 1923 were particularly important landmarks for the author. But his understanding of current issues was informed by ancient Egyptian history and especially by the view that the pharaonic past determined, to a large extent, the way Egyptians think and view the world. Al-Hakim was so convinced that the notions of time and space were uniquely essential concepts for the Egyptians that he explored these ideas in his artistic work: in the four-act play, *The People of the Cave*; in the drama, *Shahrazad*; and in the romantic novel set during the 1919 revolution, *The Return of the Soul*. Like his colleagues, al-Hakim also produced Islamic-oriented works in the 1930s: a play on the life of Muhammad and many essays on religion.

Although French had historically been the language and culture of a large section of the Egyptian aristocracy, English literature and scholarship also attracted some members of the Egyptian intelligentsia. The works of Shakespeare, Carlyle, Dickens, Tennyson, and Shaw were particularly important to

such writers as Abbas Mahmud al-Aqqad (1899–1965) and Ibrahim Abd al-Qadir al-Mazini (d. 1945).

Al-Aqqad was born in Aswan into a family of middle income.
Largely self-taught, he became a schoolteacher and made an important contribution to modern Arabic literature. At the school,
he met al-Mazini with whom he began to collaborate on articles
and volumes of poetry. Both men were modern poets whose
verses were subjective and concentrated on feelings, emotions,
and beliefs. Along with their associate Abd al-Rahman Shukri,
they criticized traditional Arab poets, their methods and their
messages. Like all Egyptian modernists, they looked forward enthusiastically to a literary revival and a nationalist renaissance.

Al-Aqqad was an idealist whose notions of freedom and truth
underlined his writings. He believed, for example, that literature
and the arts were the highest expressions of freedom and thus of
basic importance to society. Literature must do more than just
entertain readers; it must enlighten and instruct them. Al-Aqqad
was also keenly interested in politics. After World War I, he
became one of the ideological spokesmen for the Wafd and regularly wrote columns on art, literature, philosophy, religion, and
history in the party's daily newspaper, *al-Balagh*. In a book he
published in which he stubbornly defended democracy and constitutionalism, he attacked both Sidqi Pasha and the king for
jointly obstructing self-government in Egypt. For this, he was
arrested and imprisoned for nine months.

This writer's idealism, however, began to wane in the 1930s,
and he grew more conservative and more attached to religion.
Unlike his contemporary Taha Husayn, al-Aqqad considered the
1936 Anglo-Egyptian Treaty to be a betrayal of the Wafd's nationalist aspirations and a symbol of the party's moderation. He
asserted that the Wafd's consenting to limited independence
epitomized the leadership's separation from the people and signified the party's naked self-interest in attaining political power.
In 1938, al-Aqqad dropped out of the Wafd and joined the Saadist
party. After that time and consistent with his attachment to

Islam, he wrote a book about the prophet Muhammad that was published during World War II.

Another prominent Egyptian intellectual, Salama Musa, was also influenced by the English tradition of thought. Musa differed significantly from al-Aqqad and al-Mazini in that he was a Fabian Socialist whose ideas and interests derived from Shaw, H. G. Wells, Ibsen, Nietzsche, and Tolstoy. An ardent Egyptian nationalist, Musa insisted that political independence could only work if it were coupled with social change and an improvement in the quality of life for the masses. Musa respected Western culture and believed that Egypt needed to renovate itself using the West as a model. He especially favored introducing secular education, modern industry, and a scientific culture. Along with other language scholars, Musa advocated a Latinized alphabet and the replacement of literary Arabic by the vernacular. Salama Musa published many works. Some of his more controversial ones dealt with his defense of the theory of evolution and his advocacy of socialism, a theory that he believed could best solve Egypt's social and economic problems.

Like Salama Musa, other Egyptian reformers were concerned about the future of the country. An appeal for national rejuvenation was made soon after the conclusion of the 1936 treaty (though not necessarily by Socialists). In particular, two books published in 1938 provided plans for national renewal through social and economic reform. Mirrit Boutros Ghali's *The Policy of Tomorrow* and Hafiz al-Afifi's *On the Margin of Politics* have been considered the first works by Egyptians to apply a social-scientific, critical analysis to Egypt. In depicting the social and economic problems facing the country and portraying the miseries of everyday life, Ghali and al-Afifi denounced governmental inattention and condemned ruling-class contempt for the masses.

Books, poems, and short stories about workers and peasants began to appear more frequently in the 1940s. Mustafa Mahmud Fahmi, in a genre similar to that of Ghali and al-Afifi, wrote *The Social Situation in Egypt* (1940). Concentrating on the social and material condition of workers and their relations with employers, he concluded that in order to redress the imbalance between labor and management, workers must be protected from the arbitrariness of industrialists, safeguarded against industrial accidents, and assured health care, insurance, and family benefits.

In Ahmad Sadiq Saad's *The Problem of the Fallah* (1945), the conditions of the peasant, the problems of the agricultural economy, and the system of monopoly were treated from a Marxist perspective. According to Sadiq Saad, the problem of the peasant was caused by two related circumstances: the uncontrolled and unscrupulous behavior of large landowners, who dominated every aspect of rural life, and the social and economic effects of imperialism that retarded growth and development.

In addition to nonfiction, novels have appealed to the Egyptian reading audience from the beginning of the twentieth century. The works of Naguib Mahfuz, who recently won the Nobel Prize for literature, have been especially popular. In the way Tawfiq al-Hakim wrote about the 1920s and 1930s, Mahfuz masterfully produced stories about Cairo in the 1940s. He has portrayed the monotony of life among the petty bourgeoisie, and he has written poignantly and sympathetically about the poor, with all their sufferings and humiliations. Issam al-Din Hifni Nasif's work also captured the imagination of leftist activists, and the novels of Albert Cossery, in French, have appealed to cosmopolitan intellectuals.

Albert Cossery's example is particularly interesting. Born in Egypt in 1913 to Greek Catholic parents of Syrian origin, he was French educated and cultured. When he began writing novels, his literature focused on the lives of the poor, the disenfranchised, the alienated, and the dispossessed of the country. Through his literature one gets an appreciation of the lives of the inarticulate. Paradoxically, however, the language in which he worked and published was French. Cossery's bilingualism placed him, and others like him, in two psychic and cultural worlds—worlds that held irreconcilable conflicts. He was writing about Egypt's poor but using the language of the foreigner. In an important sense, Cossery was an internal exile in Egypt, mainly because he wrote, thought, and lived in a language that differed from the majority of the population. Eventually, in the mid-1940s, Cossery voluntarily emigrated to Paris.

The condition of expatriation had a paradoxical effect on Albert Cossery and his work. Although it resulted in a forfeiture of first-hand contact with the lived experience of his characters, expatriation allowed Cossery to approach his subject in a detached, deliberate, and realist way, free from the bonds of home and its proscriptions. He abandoned his marginal status in Egypt that was conditioned by his class, his ethnicity, and his Western education. In Paris, he has continued to write about what was most clearly imprinted on his memory—about the experiences and reminiscences of his youth and young adulthood. Through expatriation, Cossery gained a sense of himself and appropriated his lost culture.

Conclusion

A diversity of ideas was advanced in this period, and a range of books were published, suggesting that intellectual expression was fundamentally unrestricted. Through the political tracts made available, the historical, philosophical, and religious texts written, and the literature produced, intellectual Egyptians sought to comprehend the significance of their national experience and especially to reconcile Egyptian culture with Western civilization. In contemplating such issues, Egyptians were engaged in a discourse that allowed for proposals and solutions covering a wide spectrum of ideas. The heterogeneity and creativity of thought mark this period as a minor renaissance in Egyptian cultural development.

[8]
Conclusion

Egypt's first experience with constitutional government came in 1866 when Khedive Ismail formed the Consultative Assembly of Delegates. Modeled on European representative institutions, the assembly was composed of seventy-five delegates who were elected indirectly for three-year terms. This group was constituted to serve the practical needs of the Khedive, not because an indigenous constitutional movement demanded representation. Suffering from financial indebtedness, Ismail needed to raise taxes and wanted local support for an unpopular proposal.

Delegates were elected in 1869, 1876, and 1881. Then during the British occupation, new political chambers came into being. In 1883, the Legislative Council was formed that was composed of thirty members, fourteen of whom were nominated by the Khedive and permanent and sixteen of whom were indirectly elected for six years. At the same time, the General Assembly was established that included the Khedive's ministers, the members of the Legislative Council, and forty-six other representatives elected for periods of six years. In 1913, the Legislative Assembly was organized that consisted of seventeen indirectly elected and sixty-six nominated members.

The assemblies rarely operated autonomously. With legislative loyalty to the palace a virtual prerequisite for admittance and restrictions placed on these institutions by both the Khedive and the British, independent action was crippled. Still, these institutions were significant, not so much in the actual decisions taken, but in the educational lessons offered. A narrow segment of

Egyptian society was brought into the decision-making process and was given an appreciation of participatory politics.

The Egyptian legislators, whose numbers were small, came largely from the new class of educated men whose familiarity with the West made them natural carriers of the ideas of nationalism and constitutionalism. Through education and experience, these men were exposed to European society and were aware of the revolutionary changes brought about with the advent of democracy, scientific innovation, and industrial advance. For those in Egypt observing the West's development, the liberal system of government was considered at least partially responsible for Europe's level of progress. Fueled by an ideology of political rights and responsibilities, the West was admired by Egyptian secular reformers who looked forward to a time when Egypt could rid itself of religious conservatism and political authoritarianism.

Despite Britain's occupation of Egypt in 1882 and the decisive role the British Foreign Office played in Egyptian politics over the next seventy years, an important and informed section of the Egyptian population by the turn of the twentieth century advocated secular, rational reform based on Western liberal principles, insisting that the western system of government was essential for building a modern state and for restraining the arbitrary acts of the monarch. Thus, Egyptian society moved into a new era characterized by new systems of thought and political practice. In essence, the country constructed a political strategy based on European parliamentarianism in the hope that the progress achieved in the West could similarly be attained in Egypt. Accordingly, along with the Constitution—granted by the British in 1923—the principles of constitutionalism, individual civil rights, and democracy were introduced into Egypt, and a Western-style political structure was brought into the country.

Regrettably, the Egyptian political leadership adopted the system of European liberal democracy without shaping it to the realities and specificities of Egyptian social and political life. In Europe, the ideas of liberalism were forwarded and supported, at least initially, by members of middle-class society, those people who were self-consciously individualistic and highly productive in business and the professions. Barred from the highest echelons of aristocratic society by the lack of a title, they were encouraged to cultivate their talents and excel through hard work and determination. Democracy was a means through which their voices would be heard and their economic interests safeguarded. In Egypt, where constitutionalism was still controlled by a European power that periodically interfered in the country's political life and where the monarch enjoyed disproportionate power, unfettered liberal development was highly problematic, and the country's newly constituted democratic system faced major disadvantages. Egypt never resolved how to temper a monarch who distrusted liberalism; its leaders never addressed the problem of how to engage a traditional and highly illiterate population and bring people into the center of the political process. In reality, the political hierarchy never grappled with how "liberal" the liberal democratic system should really be. Because these questions were not squarely faced at the outset, there was never any vehicle for confronting them later as events unfolded.

If the British occupation and the antidemocratic tendencies of the monarchy hindered constitutionalism, then the social, economic, and political conditions within Egypt posed additional serious difficulties for the nascent parliamentary system. In particular, the country lacked a strong middle-class population with political muscle. As a result, agrarian-based political forces dominated the legislative arena and mandated policy at the behest of an entrenched, conservative landed elite. Arguably, had a stronger middle class existed, it might have acted in defense of democratic practice for its own class interests. Moreover, it might have tried to disable the highly placed agricultural landlords who regularly disrupted the course of liberalism and might have succeeded in reducing their hegemonic political control.

Furthermore, unlike the European democratic experience, the Egyptian experiment was not protected by pressure groups whose increasing strength and importance could have forced the ruling class to adhere faithfully to the Constitution and to the practice of political pluralism. Experimentation with liberalism in Egypt came at a time when the country was just beginning to evolve a conscious working class active in labor unions, able to articulate political demands, and able to insist upon governmental accountability. Democratic practice was brought into the country when Egyptian entrepreneurs were still dominated by the foreign and minority capitalists resident in the country and only beginning to embark on their own struggle for economic independence. In essence, because Egypt lacked an influential and indeed broad-based populace able to defend constitutional concepts and curb the power of the state, democracy in Egypt could be, and regularly was, arbitrarily manipulated by absolutist political leaders or by the antidemocratic tendencies of the monarchs and their clients. Inevitably, irreparable shocks were sent to the democratic system, and the liberal parliamentary government could not be sustained.

A structural problem was the most important cause of the failure of the Egyptian democratic experiment, though much of the literature of the period obscures the systemic weaknesses and the ambiguous attitudes of legislators. The practitioners of constitutionalism and the architects of party politics were in reality not committed to opening up the democratic system to the majority of the population. The issue was not, as Saad Eddin Ibrahim candidly states,[1] whether the people were ready for democracy but whether the ruling elite was ready for popular participation in the system. In the first half of the twentieth century, the elites evidently saw no advantage in organizing and politicizing the mass of society, except possibly in connection with the national question. What could the elites have gained from empowering the lower classes, and what could they have lost? Very likely, the elites were concerned that their hegemonic control would be threatened as people with more radical social and political views entered the political arena.

Because many of liberalism's so-called practitioners—those people who ran in elections, served in Parliament, and made policy—were not committed to allowing the system to become truly democratic, whole groups of people were cut off from the political center and thus considered themselves unrepresented. Political officials were criticized for serving narrow interests and being most concerned with their own political self-preservation. Separated from the popular classes by culture, class origin, education, expectations, and sometimes even language, these political officials commonly created elite political parties that essentially expressed their own views and were not structured to recruit members from the humbler social groups. Even the Wafd, which could have broadened its base, educated the population, and involved more people in the political process, refrained from so doing. In consequence, Egyptian liberal democracy developed in a fragmented and uneven manner with most political leaders jealous of their positions and uneasy about potential popular activity.

That Egyptians from the petty bourgeoisie, the bourgeoisie, and the working classes participated in the political arena is in fact a testament to the will of the people to become involved in politics. Voting in sporadic general elections—almost exclusively casting their votes for the Wafd—and associating with the Muslim Brotherhood, Young Egypt, the Communist movement, and the Wafdist Vanguard, they made themselves part of Egypt's political culture. Particularly noticeable as demonstrators, as protesters at the palace, as marchers through the streets, and as strikers at factories, people outside the political center were active and articulating a message. In the period from the early 1920s to the early 1950s, Egyptian political culture was diverse, reflecting contrasting ideological approaches and a variety of political behaviors. Egypt's rich political experience was attributable not only to the politically entrenched and powerful but also to the more dispossessed, to those who were not merely passive recipients of political dogma or ideological rhetoric but who were participant, active, and interested. Although the people's movements may have been defeated, their campaigns ignored, and their demands unsatisfied, their conduct demonstrated increasing political sophistication and rising aspirations.

Democracy as a theory, however, was clearly not relevant to Egyptians, despite their increased political activity. But the intensity of this activity indicates that the practice of Egyptians sharing in the political process was meaningful. This significance was demonstrated by consistent electoral activity, unrelenting nationalist fervor, and periodic interventions in the country's political life when demands for an improvement in the quality of life were given voice.

Both politically and economically, however, Egyptians were disappointed by their officials and by the philosophy of liberalism that these leaders came to represent. After repeated violations of the system in the form of rigged or canceled elections, unpopular palace-appointed cabinets, corruption, police repression against nonmainstream political forces, and occasional press censorship, constitutional practice simply lost its legitimacy. When it became clear that the liberal system had failed to serve as a catalyst for solving the burning issues of the day, people endorsed a new leadership (after 1952) that embraced radically different ideas and methods of rule. That the Egyptian population affirmed a military government whose ideological underpinnings were hostile to liberalism should not be understood as an affirmation of authoritarianism or absolutism. Rather, many in Egypt drew the conclusion that liberalism as practiced in Cairo appeared only to reinforce ruling-class hegemony and strengthen the interests of the elite. When the liberal regime ultimately broke down, the cause was the dichotomy that existed between what the people hoped for and what they got from their rulers.

For the more politically sophisticated, reconciling the inherent contradiction of adopting a European ideology at a time of European colonialism became increasingly difficult. As the theory of liberalism gradually lost its attraction, especially during the

1930s and 1940s, nonparliamentary forces argued more convincingly for Islamic fundamentalism, communism, or fascism. These ideas were also favorably received by lower middle-class and some working-class Egyptians who were well aware of being involuntarily dominated by Great Britain. In their view, Britain was a nationalist power that enforced democracy at home but refused to allow it to develop unimpeded in Egypt. Although cherishing its own patriotism, Britain was unwilling to free its colony from the yoke of colonialism.

By the outbreak of World War II, liberalism had been unable to produce true representative government, political freedom, and civil rights. The old order was being criticized by politically conscious workers, students, and young professionals whose demands for social and economic reform grew louder and more radical, especially from 1945 to 1952. Discontent was articulated through increased labor strikes, recurrent street protests, the distribution of antiestablishment handbills, and an oppositional press that voiced general disillusionment with the ruling establishment. Typically nonparliamentary forces such as the Communists, the Muslim Brotherhood, and Young Egypt, in particular, contributed to the destabilization of the government by attacking the regime and creating an environment where liberalism could be legitimately denounced.

Finally, on July 23, 1952, a small, secretive, politically diverse military group called the Free Officers carried out a coup d'etat that put an end to liberal democracy in Egypt. This group was a clandestine oppositional movement within the military with supporters from most of the political trends in Egypt, including Communists, Muslim Brothers, and nationalists. Though of different ideologies, the officers agreed on a limited number of policies that included the destruction of the monarchy, the end of British colonialism, the abolition of Egyptian-style feudalism, and the establishment of "social justice." In the early years of the new regime, the focus of domestic attention was on winning national independence and stimulating modernization. The de-

mocratizing of Egypt's economic and social life figured into the
Free Officers' program mainly as a corollary of the group's other
two aims, which can be summarized as the forming of a strong
and independent nation.

The Free Officers, who were renamed the Revolutionary Command Council (RCC), unequivocally controlled the army. But as
young, unknown, low-level officers, they had no political roots in
society. In an effort to legitimize their authority throughout the
country and gain support for their revolution, they appointed
established political figures to run the government. General Muhammad Naguib, a prominent nationalist hero, was given the
presidency of the RCC, and Ali Mahir, an anti-British politician,
was asked to lead the cabinet.

From the outset, two bailiwicks of power existed: the army and
the civilian government. Because each wanted ultimate political
authority, conflict could not be averted. During the first two
years of the revolution, a political and ideological battle waged
between the Nasserites, who supported strong military rule, and
the parliamentarians led by Naguib, who demanded the restoration of constitutional life. This ultimately became a struggle for
supreme power in Egypt. After some personal and political set-
backs, Nasser was able to convince important sections of the
military that the revolution was in grave danger and that only
his vision of the future merited support. Nasser prevailed in the
end, and by the summer of 1954, the course of the revolution was
firmly established. The Constitution had been abrogated, independent political parties were forbidden, the militarization of the
government was stepped up, and Nasser's battle for single-party
rule was triumphant. With the end of the colonial state came an
end to the political liberties that had been previously enjoyed by
most segments of the Egyptian population. Nasser, who was
heralded for his role in bringing independence to Egypt, did so
by replacing a semiliberal society with a closed and politically
uniform community.

The new leaders distanced themselves from the ancien régime

by deposing the king, mandating agricultural reform that broke the political, social, and economic power of the landlords, and terminating the system of political democracy. When political parties were banned (January 1953),[2] a government organization known as Liberation Rally was established to fill the gap left by the absence of partisan politics. Negotiations with the British were in progress during 1953–1954, and by October 1954, an agreement was reached securing Egypt's full independence. The parties agreed that all British troops were to be withdrawn within twenty months from their bases in the Suez Canal Zone and that British troops could be reactivated in the event of an attack by an outside power on an Arab League state or on Turkey. Although this latter provision received mixed reviews in Egypt because it effectively aligned the country to Western defense interests, the treaty was seen as finally closing the chapter on colonialist control of Egypt.

With the problem of the British resolved and Nasser in full charge, the regime began to conduct an independent foreign policy. Nasser went to the Bandung Conference in Indonesia in 1955 and became one of the most prominent spokesmen of positive neutralism, which was essentially a policy of nonalignment. Bandung represented a significant breakthrough for the Third World countries trying to forge a path independent of the Soviet Union and the United States. The superpowers, becoming deeply involved in the Cold War, found their efforts to mold a bipolar world breaking down as newly independent states began to exert a force in world affairs.

Egypt came into conflict with the United States after Nasser concluded an arms deal with Czechoslovakia that brought Egypt closer to the countries of the Eastern Bloc. When the United States' promise to fund the building of the Aswan Dam was withdrawn, Nasser turned to the Soviet Union for aid and then nationalized the Suez Canal Company (which was being administered by an international agency) and took over the administration of the canal. Angered by Nasser's act, Britain, France, and

Israel invaded Egypt but were forced to withdraw after the United States and the Soviet Union lodged protests in the United Nations. Nasser also became active in Arab affairs and initiated an alliance among all Arabs under Egypt's leadership. Through Nasser, Egypt was brought decisively into the Arab world where, during his lifetime, it remained the most important country in the region.

Nasser was, first and foremost, a nationalist and a patriot. Although his vision of guiding Egypt toward independent modernization went largely unfulfilled, he was highly regarded at home and within the Middle East. His popularity as a leader derived from his ability to bring dignity and self-esteem to his people, but he did so by unapologetically controlling a politically uniform society totally devoid of liberal institutions, democracy, and civic freedoms.

Notes
Selected Bibliography
Index

Notes

1. Introduction

1. Constitutional democracy in the Western world also helped to generate a bourgeois class, further encouraging the political process to develop.

2. Perhaps even more than the premodern European family.

3. Rugh, *Family Life in Contemporary Egypt*, 45; Ibrahim, "The Socio-Economic Requisites of Democracy," 59.

2. The Egyptians

1. For more information on the changing status of women during Muhammad Ali's rule, see Tucker, *Women in Nineteenth Century Egypt*.

2. For more details, see Issawi, *Egypt: An Economic and Social Analysis*.

3. Occupation and the Nationalist Response

1. Goldschmidt, *Modern Egypt*, 56; Hourani, *Arabic Thought in the Liberal Age*, 193–221.

2. Gershoni and Jankowski, *Egypt, Islam, and the Arabs*, 42.

3. Goldschmidt, *Modern Egypt*, 58.

4. Gershoni and Jankowski, *Egypt, Islam, and the Arabs*, 54.

5. The system of Capitulations, which had operated since Ottoman times, encouraged westerners to invest in and do business in Ottoman territories. Extraterritorial status exempted Europeans from local laws and tax obligations and allowed them to be tried by their own consular courts.

6. Youssef, "The Democratic Experience in Egypt," 26.

7. The author wishes to thank Zachary Lockman for his comments on the subject.

8. Binder, *In a Moment of Enthusiasm*, 39.

9. Beinin and Lockman, *Workers on the Nile*, 161–162.

10. For information on this period, see Marsot, *Egypt's Liberal Experiment*.

11. This observation was made by Marsot in *A Short History of Modern Egypt*, 85.

12. Binder, *In a Moment of Enthusiasm*, 125–127.

13. Egyptians were proud of their pharaonic past, and this connection could be exploited by political leaders.

14. Beinin and Lockman, *Workers on the Nile*, 286.

15. Naguib, *Egypt's Destiny*, 78.

16. See al-Barawi, *The Military Coup in Egypt*, Lacouture and Lacouture, *Egypt in Transition*, and Shuhdi Atiya al-Shafii, *Tatawwur al-haraka al-wataniyya al-misriyya, 1882–1956* (Cairo, 1956), for more details.

17. Tariq al-Bishri, *al-Haraka al-siyasiyya fi misr* (Cairo, 1972), 100–101.

18. Hetata, *The Eye with an Iron Lid*, 172.

19. For a detailed analysis of this last Wafdist period, see Gordon, "The False Hopes of 1950," 193–214.

20. See, for example, Jamal al-Sharqawi, *Hariq al-qahira* (Cairo, 1976), 866–69, and Muhammad Anis, *Hariq al-qahira fi 26 yanayir 1952 ala dawi wathaiq tunshar li-awwal marra* (Beirut, 1972).

21. The Socialist party, formerly Young Egypt, espoused a xenophobic message.

4. The Era of Liberal Politics

1. Binder, *In a Moment of Enthusiasm*, 39.

2. Ahmad Sadiq Saad, *Safahat min al-yasar al-misri* (Cairo, 1976), 29.

3. Deeb, *Party Politics in Egypt*, 69, 163.

4. al-Bishri, *al-Haraka al-siyasiyya fi misr*, 156–57.

5. The tarbush, sometimes known as the fez, was a felt hat, usually red in color with a black tassel.

6. al-Bishri, *al-Haraka al-siyasiyya fi misr*, 165–73.

7. Deeb, *Party Politics in Egypt*, 77; Marsot, *Egypt's Liberal Experiment*, 65.

8. Marsot, *Egypt's Liberal Experiment*, 66.

9. Deeb, *Party Politics in Egypt*, 357–66.

10. For more information, see my book, *The Rise of Egyptian Communism*.

11. For the life of Salama Musa, see Egger, *A Fabian in Egypt*.

5. The Economic and Social Setting

1. Baer, *A History of Landownership in Modern Egypt*, 77–79; Issawi, *Egypt at Mid-Century*, 127.

2. Asim al-Disuqi, *Kibar mullak al-aradi al-zira'iyya wa dawruhum fi al-mujtama al-misri, 1914–1952* (Cairo, 1975), 220.

3. I am referring here to Syrians, Jews, and Greeks who were considered foreign by much of the population and who often considered themselves as such.

4. The ethnic breakdown of the population in 1937 was as follows: Muslims, 14,522,670; Copts, 1,085,280; other Christians, 218,690; Jews, 62,950; and others, 1,070.

5. Jean Pierre Thieck, "La journée du 21 Fevrier 1946 dans l'histoire du mouvement national Égyptien" (Diplome d'études supérieures en histoire, Université de Paris VIII, 1974), 38.

6. Issawi, *Egypt at Mid-Century*, 262–63.

7. For a good account of the Egyptian student movement, see Abdalla, *The Student Movement and National Politics in Egypt*.

8. Tignor, *State, Private Enterprise, and Economic Change in Egypt*, 30.

9. Abdalla, *The Student Movement and National Politics in Egypt*, 46.

10. For more information on the Jewish community in Egypt, see Kramer, *The Jews in Modern Egypt*.

11. Rifaat al-Said, *Tarikh al-munazzamat al-yasariyya al-misriyya, 1940–1950* (Cairo, 1976), 274.

12. For a detailed institutional history of the Egyptian trade-union movement, see Beinin and Lockman, *Workers on the Nile*.

13. Deeb, "Labor and Politics in Egypt," 187–203.

14. Berque, *Egypt*, 493–94.

15. Abou Alam, *The Labor Movement in Egypt*, 9.

16. Abd al-Mun'im al-Ghazzali, *Tarikh al-haraka al-niqabiyya al-misriyya, 1889–1952* (Cairo, 1968), 217.

17. Great Britain, Foreign Office, 371/46003 J2962/440/16, September 1, 1945, Public Records Office, London.

18. Mitchell, *The Society of Muslim Brothers*, 277–82.

19. For more information on this new kind of women's journalism, see Baron, "The Rise of a New Literary Culture."

6. Religion and Politics: The Battle of Conflicting Ideologies

1. Gibb, *Mohammedanism*, 65.

2. Esposito, *Islam: The Straight Path*, 183–84.

3. For a fuller analysis of Muhammad Abduh, see Hourani, *Arabic Thought in the Liberal Age*, 130–60.

4. Esposito, *Islam and Politics*, 47–48.

5. Vatikiotis, *The Modern History of Egypt*, 329.

6. Harris, *Nationalism and Revolution in Egypt*, 146.

7. See Mitchell, *The Society of Muslim Brothers*, and Esposito, *Islam: The Straight Path*, for a fuller discussion.

8. Mitchell, *The Society of Muslim Brothers*, 71.

9. Esposito, *Islam: The Straight Path*, 157–61.

10. The discussion of the Egyptian Communist movement has been excerpted from my articles that appeared in *Studies in Comparative Communism* 18, no. 1 (Spring 1985):49–65, and *Journal of South Asian and Middle Eastern Studies* 10, no. 3 (Spring 1987):78–94. For a fuller account of the Communist movement, see my study, *The Rise of Egyptian Communism*.

11. Fuad Mursi, interview with author, Cairo, November 12, 1979.

12. For a fascinating biography of Henri Curiel, see Perrault, *A Man Apart*.

13. Raymond Stambouli, interview with author, Paris, June 4, 1980.
14. Sharif Hatata, interview with author, Cairo, February 28, 1980.

7. Cultural Expression in Egypt

1. For a more comprehensive discussion of these writers, see Hourani, *Arabic Thought in the Liberal Age*, Safran, *Egypt in Search of Political Community*, and Gershoni and Jankowski, *Egypt, Islam, and the Arabs*.
2. Quoted in Safran, *Egypt in Search of Political Community*, 153–54.
3. The caliph was the head of the Islamic community after Muhammad, inheriting the social and political functions of the Prophet and acting as the final arbiter in any dispute. By the tenth century, however, the office of the caliphate had declined in importance. The Ottomans later decided to restore the position in their empire. The ruling sultan—as leader of the Islamic community—incorporated the prestige and mission of the caliphate, but, in addition, his voice in secular matters was authoritative. The abolition of the caliphate by Mustafa Kemal stirred up hostility among Muslims throughout the world. Efforts to revive the caliphate have been consistently unsuccessful.
4. Quoted in Hourani, *Arabic Thought in the Liberal Age*, 326.
5. Quoted in Safran, *Egypt in Search of Political Community*, 176.
6. Ibid., 178.

8. Conclusion

1. Ibrahim, "The Socio-Economic Requisites of Democracy," 55–56.
2. The Muslim Brotherhood, which was considered a religious organization, was allowed to function until it too was banned in January 1954.

Selected Bibliography

Abdalla, Ahmed. *The Student Movement and National Politics in Egypt*. London: Al-Saqi Books, 1985.

Abdel-Malek, Anouar. *Egypt: Military Society, the Army Regime, the Left, and Social Change under Nasser*. New York: Random House, 1968.

Abou Alam, Abdel Raouf. *The Labor Movement in Egypt*. Washington, D.C.: Egyptian Embassy, 1955.

Ahmed, Jamal M. *The Intellectual Origins of Egyptian Nationalism*. London: Oxford University Press, 1960.

Anis, Muhammad. *Hariq al-qahira fi 26 yanayir 1952 ala dawi wathaiq tunshar li-awwal marra*. Beirut, 1972.

Baer, Gabriel. *A History of Landownership in Modern Egypt, 1800–1950*. London: Oxford University Press, 1963.

al-Barawi, Rashed. *Economic Development in the U.A.R*. Cairo: Anglo-Egyptian Bookshop, 1970.

———. *The Military Coup in Egypt*. Cairo: Renaissance Publishers, 1952.

Baron, Beth. "The Rise of a New Literary Culture: The Women's Press of Egypt, 1892–1919." Ph.D. diss., University of California, Los Angeles, 1988.

Beinin, Joel, and Zachary Lockman. *Workers on the Nile: Nationalism, Communism, Islam, and the Egyptian Working Class, 1882–1954*. Princeton University Press, 1987.

Berque, Jacques. *Egypt: Imperialism and Revolution*. Translated by Jean Stewart. London: Faber, 1972.

Binder, Leonard. *In a Moment of Enthusiasm: Political Power and the Second Stratum in Egypt*. Chicago: University of Chicago Press, 1978.

al-Bishri, Tariq. *al-Haraka al-siyasiyya fi misr, 1945–1952*. Cairo, 1972.

Botman, Selma. *The Rise of Egyptian Communism, 1939–1970*. Syracuse: Syracuse University Press, 1988.

Cole, Juan. "Feminism, Class, and Islam in Turn-of-the-Century Egypt." *International Journal of Middle East Studies* 13 (1981):387–407.

Colombe, Marcel. *L'evolution de l'Egypte, 1924–1950*. Paris: Maisonneuve, 1951.

Dahl, Robert A. *Democracy, Liberty and Equality*. Oxford: Oxford University Press, 1986.

———. *A Preface to Democratic Theory*. Chicago: University of Chicago Press, 1956.

Davis, Eric. *Challenging Colonialism: Bank Misr and Egyptian Industrialization, 1920–1941.* Princeton, N.J.: Princeton University Press, 1983.

Deeb, Marius. *Party Politics in Egypt: The Wafd and Its Rivals, 1919–1939.* London: Ithaca Press, 1979.

———. "Labor and Politics in Egypt: 1919–1939." *International Journal of Middle East Studies* 10 (May 1979):187–203.

———. "The 1919 Popular Uprising: A Genesis of Egyptian Nationalism." *Canadian Review of Studies in Nationalism* 1 (1973):106–119.

Egger, Vernon. *A Fabian in Egypt: Salamah Musa and the Rise of the Professional Classes in Egypt, 1909–1939.* Lanham, Md.: University Press of America, 1986.

Esposito, John. *Islam and Politics.* Syracuse: Syracuse University Press, 1984.

———. *Islam: The Straight Path.* New York: Oxford University Press, 1988.

Gershoni, Israel, and James Jankowski. *Egypt, Islam, and the Arabs: The Search for Egyptian Nationhood, 1900–1930.* New York: Oxford University Press, 1986.

Ghali, Mirrit Boutros. *The Policy of Tomorrow.* Washington, D.C.: Egyptian Embassy, 1953.

Gibb, H. A. R. *Mohammedanism.* London: Oxford University Press, 1975.

Goldschmidt, Arthur. *Modern Egypt: The Formation of a Nation-State.* Boulder, Colo.: Westview Press, 1988.

Gordon, Joel. "The False Hopes of 1950: The Wafd's Last Hurrah and the Demise of Egypt's Old Order." *International Journal of Middle East Studies* 21 (May 1989):193–214.

Gran, Peter. "Modern Trends in Egyptian Historiography: A Review Article." *International Journal of Middle East Studies* 9 (August 1978): 367–71.

Harris, Christina Phelps. *Nationalism and Revolution in Egypt.* Stanford, Calif.: Hoover Institution Press, 1964.

Hetata, Sharif. *The Eye with an Iron Lid.* London: Onyx Press, 1982.

Hourani, Albert. *Arabic Thought in the Liberal Age, 1798–1939.* London: Oxford University Press, 1970.

Ibrahim, Saad Eddin. "The Socio-Economic Requisites of Democracy." In *Democracy in Egypt,* edited by Ali Hillal Dessouki. Cairo Papers in Social Science. Cairo: American University Press, 1978.

Issawi, Charles. *Egypt: An Economic and Social Analysis.* London: Oxford University Press, 1947.

———. *Egypt at Mid-Century.* London: Oxford Univeristy Press, 1954.

———. *Egypt in Revolution: An Economic Analysis.* London: Oxford University Press, 1963.

Jankowski, James. *Egypt's Young Rebels: "Young Egypt," 1933–1952.* Stanford, Calif.: Hoover Institution Press, 1975.

Kotb, Sayyid. *Social Justice in Islam.* Translated by John Hardie. Washington, D.C.: American Council of Learned Societies, 1953.

Kramer, Gudrun. *The Jews in Modern Egypt, 1914–1952.* Seattle: University of Washington Press, 1989.

Lacouture, Jean, and Simonne Lacouture. *Egypt in Transition.* Translated by Francis Scarfe. New York: Criterion, 1958.

Lipset, Seymour M. *Political Man: The Social Bases of Politics.* Rev. ed. Baltimore: Johns Hopkins University Press, 1981.

Louis, Roger. *The British Empire in the Middle East, 1945–1951.* New York: Oxford University Press, 1984.

Mansfield, Peter. *The British in Egypt.* New York: Holt, Rinehart and Winston, 1971.

Marsot, Afaf Lutfi al-Sayyid. *Egypt's Liberal Experiment, 1922–1936.* Berkeley: University of California Press, 1977.

————. "The Revolutionary Gentlewomen in Egypt." In *Women in the Muslim World,* edited by Lois Beck and Nikki Keddie. Cambridge: Harvard University Press, 1978.

————. *A Short History of Modern Egypt.* Cambridge: Cambridge University Press, 1985.

Mitchell, Richard P. *The Society of Muslim Brothers.* London: Oxford University Press, 1969.

Musa, Salama. *The Education of Salama Musa.* Translated by L. O. Schuman. Leiden: Brill, 1961.

Naguib, Mohammed. *Egypt's Destiny: A Personal Statement.* Garden City, N.Y.: Doubleday, 1955.

Perrault, Gilles. *A Man Apart: The Life of Henri Curiel.* Translated by Bob Cumming. London and Atlantic Highlands, N.J.: Zed Press, 1987.

Rugh, Andrea. *Family Life in Contemporary Egypt.* Syracuse: Syracuse University Press, 1984.

Safran, Nadav. *Egypt in Search of Political Community.* Cambridge: Harvard University Press, 1961.

Smith, Charles. "4 February 1942: Its Causes and Its Influences on Egyptian Politics." *International Journal of Middle East Studies* 10 (November 1979):453–79.

Terry, Janice. *Cornerstone of Egyptian Political Power: The Wafd, 1919–1952.* London: Third World Center ,1982.

Tignor, Robert. *State, Private Enterprise, and Economic Change in Egypt, 1918–1952.* Princeton, N.J.: Princeton University Press, 1984.

Tucker, Judith. *Women in Nineteenth Century Egypt.* Cambridge: Cambridge University Press, 1985.

Vatikiotis, P. J. *The Modern History of Egypt.* London: Weidenfeld and Nicholson, 1969.

Youssef, Hassan. "The Democratic Experience in Egypt, 1923–1952." In *Democracy in Egypt,* edited by Ali Hillal Dessouki. Cairo Papers in Social Science. Cairo: American University Press, 1978.

Ziadeh, Farhat J. *Lawyers, the Rule of Law, and Liberalism in Modern Egypt.* Stanford, Calif.: Hoover Institution Press, 1968.

Index

Contemporary Issues in the Middle East

This well-established series continues to focus primarily on twentieth-century developments that have current impact and significance throughout the entire region, from North Africa to the borders of Central Asia.

Recent titles in the series include:

Egypt from Independence to Revolution, 1919–1952
was composed in 10 on 13 Palatino on a Varityper EPICS
system by Blue Heron; printed by sheet-fed offset on 60-pound
acid-free Glatfelter B-16 Natural, Smyth-sewn and bound over
binder's boards in Holliston Roxite A, and perfect bound
with paper covers printed in 2 colors by
Thomson-Shore, Inc.; designed by
Kachergis Book Design
and published by
SYRACUSE UNIVERSITY PRESS
Syracuse, New York 13244-5160

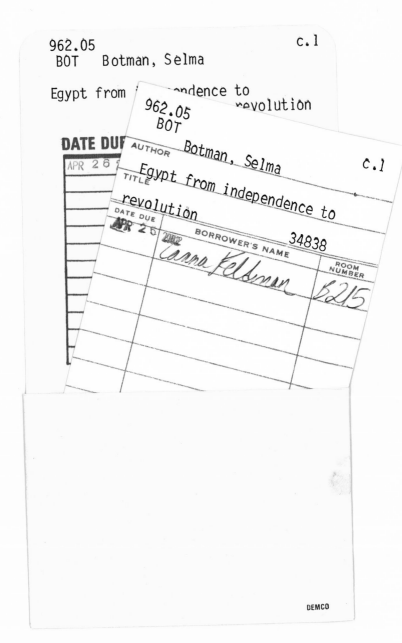